the graduate's guide™
to
MONEY

Tools for starting your financial journey on the right foot

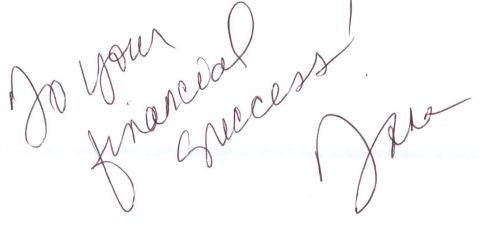

To your financial success!

Tana Ackerly Gildea CFP®, CPA

The Graduate's Guide™ to Money

Copyright © 2014 Tana Ackerly Gildea, CFP®, CPA

All Rights Reserved. Published 2014.

First published by Tana Ackerly Gildea

ISBN: 978-0-692-26590-1

Library of Congress Control Number: 2014913770

Printed in the United States of America
Tana Ackerly Gildea
4272 Highborne Drive., NE
Marietta, GA 30066

www.graduatesguidetomoney.com

Dedication

To my children, Meaghan, Ryan, Kory, and Jack, who are my inspiration and my heart.

Go forth and live a financially stress-free life!

And to my husband, Tom, who is not only the best husband in the world but the best friend.

Acknowledgements

Thank you to my husband, Tom. You are a rock: strong, committed, and dependable. I knew it the moment that I took your hand at the altar and you have never wavered. Saying "I do" was the smartest and best thing I have ever done.

To my mom, who is the most extraordinary woman I know. Thank you for guiding me through the storm. And thanks to my sisters, Raquel and Jen, who make me laugh like nobody can.

To Anita Paul, who helped me to birth this book. Without you, it would still be a file on my computer. I appreciate your insight, guidance, and (gentle) kicks in the tail when my life was pulling me away. Thank you to Katy Gillis who helped me find you.

Thank you to John and Kevin, my partners, who gave me my start and taught me everything important about the financial planning business. And thank you, Jill, who met me at a tennis match and told John to interview me.

Thank you to my readers, Cuyler Esposito, Nick Henry, Patrick Tucker, Brynn Riopelle, and Daniel Lemaux who gave their time and insights to make this a better book. Thank you to Dawn Bond and Kevin Kraus for their technical expertise and review of the facts of this book. If there are mistakes, they are all mine.

To all the writers whose words have informed me, shaped me, molded me, and sometimes saved me. Thank you for sharing your gifts with the world.

Contents

Before You Jump In: This, That, and the Other

Why Read a "Money" Book?

Nobody starts out life thinking, "I want to be in debt, live paycheck-to-paycheck, and feel financially strapped my whole life," yet that is what happens to a lot of people. There is nothing worse than feeling like you can't pay your bills. But, on the flip side, there is nothing better than feeling in control of your financial life. Having a plan and making it happen helps you feel secure and provides peace of mind. Like it or not, having money brings feelings of accomplishment and competence, and not having it brings feelings of shame and fear.

Most schools don't provide a lot of financial education, so how are you supposed to know this stuff? The reality is that talking to family members about money may be taboo, or at the very least, uncomfortable. If your relatives are in the financial ditch, you certainly don't want to take their advice! Making bad money decisions early on leads to financial worries and pressures that wreak havoc on what should be a fantastic life, so the sooner you take responsibility for your own financial security and well-being, the sooner you will create financial security.

Life is what happens while you are making other plans. Things happen. People get sick, injured, lose jobs, have setbacks. A little financial reserve can make all the difference in how you weather life's storms.

Financial differences/financial stress is the number one cause of divorce in the United States. Getting a firm grip on your own financial priorities makes discussing money with a potential spouse that much easier. If you are crystal clear on your own financial priorities and have a vision of what you want your financial life to be, you will be much more successful partnering with a spouse as you create a shared vision.

And maybe, most importantly, you don't know what you don't know. You might eventually figure it all out, but why not take a shortcut? Explore some of these financial topics before you need to know so that you are ahead of the game.

A lot of books on the market are directed at cleaning up the money mess, but not at getting started on the right foot. My hope for you is that this book helps you create a solid foundation of knowledge about the basics of money and related financial matters, gets you thinking about what is important to you, and helps you align your spending and savings around those things.

Who Am I To Be Writing This Book?

I am, first and foremost, someone who made a lot of mistakes with money in my 20s and 30s. I learned as I went. Fortunately they were never "into the ditch" mistakes, but if I could go back in time and undo some of those bad decisions, I would be much wealthier than I am now. I became a financial planner in my 40s, and I finally feel like I know what I am doing managing my money. That doesn't mean I don't spend too much on occasion or that I am perfect by any means, but I know what I am doing. I am working my own financial plan, and I hope that you can learn from some of my missteps and newly found knowledge.

I am both a Certified Public Accountant (CPA) and a CERTIFIED FINANCIAL PLANNER (CFP)®. I worked first as a CPA doing corporate audits and then as a corporate operations manager. I got the CFP® designation because my background and work experience did not give me the broad range of personal financial knowledge that I needed in order to offer the holistic financial planning experience that my firm provides.

I have four kids and I see how different their experience with money is now in the digital age than mine was in the "brick and mortar" banking world I grew up in. I see how their perception of money is different and I see that the world has become more complex. Financial education has not changed a bit though. I had none and they have none! I wanted to pour my financial knowledge and experience into their heads, but didn't have a good way to do that (my kids certainly aren't going to listen to me!). Maybe they will sneak a peek at my book, though (please!).

I am writing this book for my kids, who are soon to be adults, and for you, a newly minted graduate, because I want you to know all of the money stuff that I didn't know for the first 20 years of my adult life. I was a financial person, but I didn't know anything about personal financial matters. I hope I can save you from at least one big financial mistake in your life (hopefully lots of them!), get you started early with making a plan for yourself, and help eliminate one of the biggest sources of stress in life: money.

How To Use This Book

Use this book as Financial Planning 101, but if you need the advanced course, nothing beats advice from a qualified professional that is tailored to your situation. Until you get to that phase, here's what to do:

- Flip through this book and look at the chapters to become familiar with some of the topics that are out there in the financial world.
- Refer to the index or table of contents when a financial question arises.
- Review the chapters on employee benefits in "Your First Job" (Chapter 2), "Paying the Bills" (Chapter 3), "Income Taxes" (Chapter 6), and "Insurance" (Chapter 7). You may not think you need to understand these areas yet, but it's very helpful if you do.

- Read Chapter 12: "Money: The More You Have the Better You Like It." This is a bit more of a philosophical approach to how time, energy, effort, and money are related, so read through that and see how it compares to your own thoughts about money. Find the chapters that interest or intrigue you. You will be drawn to different topics at different times in your life. All of the information is important, yet some of the topics are more or less relevant to your situation in different phases of your life.

- Notice the terms in the footnotes. These are terms you'll need to become familiar with as your knowledge of money and finances increases.

- Most importantly, critically evaluate everything that I say and consider if that rings true for you and your situation. Very few things are absolute in this world, and you may disagree with my approach to some things. Knowing what wouldn't work for you is an important step to identifying what will.

What This Book Is

- **Financial basics:** Nobody's situation is exactly like yours; however, most people will, at some time in their lives, need most of this information—even if it's to conclude that you don't need it!

- **A financial reference book:** It's a starting point of basic situations that most people encounter. Most topics go much deeper than what's presented here, so notice the references you can use in your next phase of life.

What This Book Isn't

- **Financial advice:** Financial advice is offered all over the internet. This guide isn't designed to offer you advice. Remember, your situation is unique to you, so you have to decide which financial basics make sense for your situation.

- **The only financial information you'll ever need:** This is a starting point. While new financial products may emerge, the financial basics will always be the same.

I wish I had developed a financial plan in my 20s instead of in my 40s. I would be in a much different position than I am in today if I had developed a big picture plan. So I recommend that you at least sit down and think about some of the questions I pose in the last chapter, "What Is Your Financial Plan?" This is not the "be all, end all," but is simply meant to be a starting point to creating your own plan.

Planning for Retirement vs. Planning for Financial Independence

You might think that you will never be old, never retire, and will be rich for the rest of your life. Retirement is something your grand-parents do, right? For you, that's way off. It's so far in the future that you probably can't imagine it. Actually, retirement means financial independence, and financial independence can be for anybody at any age.

Financial independence means that you can support yourself without working. Doesn't that sound good? By planning for financial independence, you can eventually get to the point that you use your talents in the areas that you care about without concern for whether or not you get paid. If you were to start seriously saving for financial independence at age 23, you really will be rich enough to become financially independent. If everyone could live like that, the world would be a happier, safer place.

Read through Chapter 10: "Retirement Financial Independence: You Gotta Save How Much?" Make a plan to become financially independent. Your plan will evolve over the years, but if you keep the goal in mind and keep taking action, you can achieve your goal. Don't just hope for it, plan for it! Working through Chapter 14 will help you do that.

Do You Need a Financial Advisor?

As your financial life gets more complicated (as in, when you make more money), you will need a lot more financial guidance than you will find here, and that is where professional financial advisors come in. Many people need help with their finances. The smart ones seek help early. You might not think you need help as a young adult, but here are some scenarios that might lead you to require assistance in getting set up financially:

- If you make a significant amount of money right out of college or get significant bonuses, you could use a financial advisor to help you minimize taxes and get a jump start on investing and planning for financial independence.

- If you inherit money or other assets, you probably need some financial advice about how best to utilize those assets and not make expensive mistakes.

- If you have your own business, you really need a financial advisor who can help you with taxes, retirement plans, and succession planning.

- If you have children, you need to make sure that your life insurance and wills are appropriate for protecting your children. A financial advisor can help coordinate those areas as well as college planning if it is important to you to help your children pay for college.

- If you have a unique family situation, a special needs child, a disabled spouse, or other family members who rely on you financially, you must make sure that your financial life is structured to meet their needs if something happens to you.

- If you really want to create a solid financial life, it is a great idea to have a professional help you create a financial plan. Your cost for professional financial planning will be a flat fee, somewhere in the range of $1,000 – $10,000, depending on the complexity of your situation, although some advisors may charge an hourly rate.

If you fall into any of these categories, take a look at the appendix for more information about financial advisors and how to find the best one to fit your situation. It's really tough to think about paying a professional a fee that could be in the thousands of dollars when you have other priorities for your money, but if you look at it as an investment in your financial future, it is easier to swallow.

All right, that's enough odds and ends. Go forth and learn some financial stuff!

CHAPTER I

Money Story

In this chapter:

- Three-Step Process
- What Are Your Money Beliefs?
- Responsibility—The Bedrock Belief
- Habits—The Power Behind Your Beliefs

Rest assured, this isn't a long history of the greenback. Fascinating as that would be, you're probably more interested in exploring the history of you and money: the love story. It is a love story, right?

> **Money Story**—all of your ideas, feelings, beliefs, history, impressions, perceptions, experience, and learned information about money, its place in your life, and how it works in the world whether conscious or unconscious.

Following are three areas that form your money story:

- Beliefs are the often unconscious filters through which you see the world and which drive your actions.
- Responsibility is the bedrock of belief. Who do you think is responsible for your current situation? Do you think you have control or that things just happen to you?
- Habits are beliefs turned into consistent actions.

You began learning about your world subconsciously as a child. A lot of your money experiences and feelings came from childhood experiences, but your money story is shaped every time you have an experience with money. When you delve into your gut reaction—that feeling in your belly—you access the subconscious impressions of money that you picked up without even realizing you were picking them up. Maybe you asked questions and got snapped at or ridiculed by an adult. Maybe adults taught you about money in a nurturing way. There is a big difference between those two experiences that could have a huge impact on your money story. The bottom line:

- It matters whether your parents fought about money or projected confidence and tranquility around money.
- It matters if they complained about how hard money was to get or communicated the idea of abundance.
- It matters if money was very tight or was plentiful.
- It matters if people praised your ability to accumulate and manage money or criticized your efforts.
- It matters if money was discussed openly in your household or was a taboo subject.

Your every interaction with money matters as all of your past experiences have combined to form your unique money story. By thinking about your emotions regarding money, and what memories you have of money, you can consciously evaluate your money story and decide if it is a love story or a tragedy (or maybe a comedy).

The great news is that you can change your story. You can unilaterally expel bad perceptions about money and bring in new, good facts and expectations. You can understand and forgive your parents if they were dolts about money and saddled you with ridiculous notions about it. You can bring some of your perceptions out of the dark and into the light to evaluate them rationally and decide as an adult if that perception is reality and if it is serving you well or driving you into a ditch.

Beliefs—the filters through which you see, evaluate, and interact with the world. Beliefs are often:

- subconscious, unless you have reason to question or explore them
- based on perceptions rather than facts
- "borrowed" from others
- developed at a young age while you were trying to understand the world

Three-Step Process

Use this three-step process to identify your deeply held money perceptions:

Step 1: Excavate Your Money Memories

Think back to your very first memories around money. Go back before that, and back a little bit more.

- How do you feel in your gut as you consider those memories? Do you get a sick feeling or a calm feeling? Are you nervous, anxious, afraid, happy, ashamed, calm, or something else?
  - Would you characterize those early memories as positive, negative, or neutral?
  - Do you think those memories contributed to how you view money today?
- How did the adults in your life talk about people who had a lot of money? What was the conversation regarding those who were struggling financially?
- If you look at your experiences objectively, what did they teach you about money? In other words, how did those experiences impact your beliefs about money?
  - Now that you have some insights, how valid are your childhood beliefs?

- How did your experiences impact your beliefs about your ability to earn money, save it, and spend it wisely?
- And most importantly, are these beliefs accurate?
- Now that you have some insights, how valid are your childhood beliefs and impressions about money and those who have it versus those who don't? For example, to effectively earn money, you have to believe that you can earn it. You have to understand the relationship between work and pay, and you have to fundamentally believe that you have some control over the earning process. If you believe that you have to be a brown-haired male in order to earn a lot of money then you are in big trouble if you are a blonde woman! Guess how successful you will be at earning money. Not very, because your fundamental belief is flawed.

That's silly, you say. Nobody believes anything as ridiculous as you have to be a brown-haired male in order to earn a lot of money. If you have any constraints around who can earn a lot of money, then you have some flawed beliefs. Do you honestly believe that you are unlimited in your ability to earn money and that you have unlimited capacity to earn money? If you don't, why don't you believe that? What is limiting you? That is a flawed belief.

What are your limiting beliefs about your ability to earn money? Do any of these sound familiar?

- "I'm too young and have no experience." Bella Weems started Origami Owl, a successful direct sale jewelry company, at age 14. 14! What were you doing at 14?
- "I don't have much support." You have you and about a million people online who are working in the career you want and are blogging about it. You also have millions of people trying their hand at entrepreneurship and looking for support. Help someone and you will be helped.
- "I have children." Come on! There are too many successful employees and entrepreneurs with children to even begin to list them.

- "I don't have enough money." Hello, Mary Kay Ash had to ask her husband for 10 bucks in her pre-Mary Kay days. She decided she never wanted to have to ask again. She probably never did!

- "I don't have enough education." Pa-lease. You have the World Wide Web. You have access to the sum total of thousands of years of human history, knowledge, and experience. You have millions of blogs written by millions of successful people telling you exactly what they did to become successful and sharing their missteps as well as their milestones. You have Coursera.org, an online university with dozens of free courses taught by professors from dinky little places like Stanford University. You have YouTube, which is now the world's largest search engine, teaching you how to do anything and everything. Ever heard of TED talks? Yep, the largest single collection of brilliant, creative thought leaders telling you what they are thinking about . . . for free. Enough said.

Whatever excuse you toss out, there are hundreds, if not thousands, of people who have achieved their goals in spite of that. If you don't get anything out of this book, get this:

- You have absolutely unlimited capacity to earn unlimited amounts of money.
- You and only you are in complete control of the earning process.
- You have everything you need right now, this minute, to get started.

Do you see how having that belief system might positively impact your earning future? If you do not believe these things, you have to figure out why by exploring the murky depths of your subconscious. Look for the experiences, memories, or comments that have built this bad belief. You might have some flash of insight or you might have to explore and ponder this question over time to bring up the root of the belief.

If you find yourself thinking thoughts that suggest you don't have control or you don't have potential, stop yourself and ask:

- Where is that belief coming from?
- Who do I know who shares this belief? In other words, who might have "given" me this belief?

All of this is excavating the old beliefs about money. Holding them up to the light brings them into your conscious mind. Uncover the source of the belief and you can advance to the next step:

Step 2: Question Your Beliefs

Poke those beliefs with a stick and see if they squirm. Most likely, they will. Ask these questions about what you believe:

- Are your beliefs helping you or hurting you? Can you find an example where those beliefs are not true for someone else?
- Can you find an example where they are not true for you?
- How would you feel if you discovered a flaw in your beliefs? What would you do?
- Can you accept that your beliefs are flawed?

Many of the recovery programs teach that the first step to recovery is admitting your problem. So when you can admit that your beliefs around a money issue aren't working very well for you, the next step is:

Step 3: Identify Better Beliefs

Observe successful people—those you know, such as family members or coworkers, as well as those you know of, such as celebrities or business moguls—and identify some of their beliefs based on what you see outwardly. For example, it's pretty safe to say that practically everybody who is self-made started out exactly where you are. What turned things around for them was their belief that they had control over their ability to earn lots of money, and that they could overcome challenges in order to create the financial life they wanted.

Now that you've examined some of the limiting beliefs you have about money, examine the good beliefs you have around money.

What Are Your Money Beliefs?

- What do you believe about your ability to earn money?

- What do you believe about your ability to manage money?
- What do you believe about your ability to accumulate money (savings)?
- What do you believe about your ability to spend your money wisely?
- What do you believe about your ability to meet your own and your family's economic needs?
- What do you believe about your ability to invest and grow your wealth?
- What do you believe about your ability to be debt free?
- What do you believe about your ability to create financial independence for yourself?
- What do you believe about your ability to help others?
- What do you believe about your need for material things and your ability to obtain them?
- What do you believe about the gifts, skills, and abilities you have to offer the world?

Uncovering your beliefs around these areas is critical to helping you create the financial life you want. If you ever find yourself struggling with money or feeling bad about money or money decisions, check your gut and do some digging to understand your own money story and how it impacts you today. Check your gut often when you feel anxious around money and excavate the memory, question the underlying belief, and see if you can create a better belief that will help you achieve success with money.

Answer the money questions above and develop the belief system that you want to use going forward. Anchor that belief system with the philosophy that the world is an abundant place. There is plenty for everyone. You have unlimited ability to contribute to the world in a way that will create prosperity for you and your family. You have absolute control over the process.

There are rules to follow, however. There is work to do and obstacles to overcome, but you have resources and abilities that will serve you well. An attitude of gratitude for all that you have, for the amazing country you live in, and for the opportunities that abound is a firm foundation for creating other beliefs. Remember and understand your past money story so you can proactively create your future money story, one that has a prosperous, happy beginning, middle, and end.

Responsibility—The Bedrock Belief

Who is responsible for your paycheck, your debts, your account balance, and your overall situation?

The only answer is, "You are."

Your parents are not responsible for your student loans. Your employer isn't to blame because your check is so small, nor is the government at fault for taking those rotten taxes. Your current money situation is not due to the bad economy or the high cost of college. You, and only you, have to own where you are right now because your reality represents the sum total of all the choices you have made in the past. You might love your current situation, and if you do, thank all the people who helped you get there, and keep making those same kinds of decisions. If you don't like where you are now, blame only yourself.

Jim Rohn, a master in the personal success arena, calls these "philosophies of mind." I enthusiastically recommend that you read, or better yet listen to, some of his work. Google him or search Amazon or your local library for him. He is a hoot to listen to because of his unique inflections and funny sayings. He was a rip-roaring success so his advice is priceless!

When you take responsibility for every aspect of your current situation, you have taken the wheel of your life. You are in charge.

"Whether you believe you can or believe you can't, you're right."
~ Henry Ford

Habits—The Power Behind Your Beliefs

Benjamin Franklin said, "Your net worth to the world is usually determined by what remains after your bad habits are subtracted from your good ones."

What Ben was saying is that if you want to create something of value to the world, develop good habits that lead to excellence. And if you want to create a financial net worth that makes you smile instead of cry, take stock of your money habits and quickly replace the bad ones with some good ones. Control your habits and you can rule the world (or at least your corner of it). Here are a few powerful examples of areas where you can develop good or bad habits:

Spending: "It's only $10." That habit can lead to hundreds of dollars in credit card debt per month, not to mention a shortage when your bills are due.

- Underlying belief: Small amounts don't matter.
- Resulting habits: Toss lots of little stuff into the cart; stop for coffee every day.

Saving: "I'll start with saving $10 out of every paycheck." That habit can lead to hundreds of dollars saved over time.

- Underlying belief: Every little bit helps me reach my goals. Every penny matters.
- Resulting habits: Regular savings (even a little) that have a big impact in the long term.

Bottom line: Both of these examples illustrate that small amounts add up to big amounts over time when repeated consistently.

Spending and saving habits are formed the day you get that first dollar bill handed to you in the form of your first paycheck and assume responsibility for paying your own bills. What habits will you form with respect to:

- Cooking versus eating out?

- Saving versus spending on entertainment?
- Paying off credit card balances monthly versus carrying a balance?
- Saving to buy big-ticket items versus using consumer debt (financing)?
- Paying off debt versus ignoring debt?
- Using coupons or waiting for a sale versus paying full price?
- Grocery shopping from a list versus winging it when you get to the store?
- Charitable giving versus stinginess or hoarding money?
- Creating a spending plan versus seeing what's left after you pay your bills?
- Buying a used car versus buying a new car or leasing?

All of these things seem minor in the moment, but in a very short period of time, they become habits, for better or for worse. Stopping for one $5 coffee won't change your life. But it will if you do it seven days a week, twice a day. Ten bucks a day is $3,650 a year!

Do you go out to eat every weekend? You work hard; you deserve some down time, a reward for working hard all week. What is the price tag on that, week after week after week? Maybe instead, you could think that you "deserve" to have some money! How about adopting the habit of taking your lunch to work rather than eating out? That's probably another $10-bucks-a-day decision. The important thing here is to think about how you spend money unconsciously on things that may not be your highest priorities.

In Chapter 3 you'll be looking at what is most important to you and setting up a plan to align your money with your values. You do work hard, you do want to enjoy life, and you do want to be able to do things that you enjoy doing. When you consciously identify those things and allocate money to them, you ensure that there is money to do those things as well as money for longer-term goals and savings. Creating habits that line up with your priorities moves you toward them effortlessly. Creating habits that conflict with your goals and priorities moves you away from them unconsciously.

Excavate and evaluate your habits. Eliminate those that don't work for you and create new ones that will move you in the right direction. You are only 21 days away from a new habit, or so they say. So get started now!

"We are what we repeatedly do.
Excellence, then, is not an act, but a habit."
~ Aristotle

CHAPTER 2

Your First Job: You're Rich!

In this chapter:

- Forms: I-9, W-4
- Employee Benefits
- Your Paycheck
- Taxes
- Insurance
- Types of Health Plans
- Stock Plans

Congratulations! You got a "real" job. Your parents are happy and you are on your way. Your first day dawns, you show up full of excitement and anticipation, and you get . . . drum roll, please . . . paperwork! Forms, forms, and more forms, and maybe a few booklets. Maybe you get a computer screen with lots of blanks to fill in. What is all this stuff?

Forms

Form I-9: Employment Eligibility Verification

This form is used by the government to document that you are legally eligible to work in the United States. Every employer is required to have each employee complete this form. You are required to show documents that verify your U.S. citizenship and eligibility to work here.

What documents do you need to provide?

A U.S. passport proves who you are and that you are authorized to work in this country. If you don't have a passport, you can use a driver's license (proof of who you are) and a social security card (proof that you can work in the United States). For a full list of other acceptable documents, go to www.uscis.gov/files/form/i-9.pdf.

See Appendix for the I-9 and related information.

Form W-4: Employee's Withholding Allowance Certificate

This Internal Revenue Service form tells your employer how many allowances[1] you have for federal and state income tax withholding[2]. Your employer uses this to determine how much to withhold from each paycheck for your federal and state tax obligation. Yes, Uncle Sam gets his money before you get yours.

More allowances = less withholding

On the form, you indicate how many allowances you should input. If you are single, working just one job, and won't itemize[3] your deductions[4], your allowances will be 2. See Appendix for a copy of the W-4 and the related worksheets.

If you under-withhold on taxes during the year, you will pay on April 15th! Not only do you pay the tax due but you pay penalties. Ouch! More on taxes later.

---

1 Allowances: Component of the payroll tax system. Each allowance excludes a pre-set amount of an employee's income from the application of federal and state income tax for withholding purposes. It is similar to the concept of exemptions, but an allowance is not strictly tied to the number of dependents one has.

2 Withholding: Amount that an employer subtracts from an employee's paycheck and remits to the government to cover either payroll taxes or income taxes.

3 Itemize: Process of listing individual deductible items on a tax return in order to reduce taxable income. The alternative to listing these deductible items on Schedule A is to claim the standard deduction.

4 Deductions: Amount that the tax code allows taxpayers to subtract from their income prior to determining the tax due.

Employee Benefits

This is the good stuff. These are the extras that the employer provides to you (or not) as part of your employment with the company. If you work for a really big company, you'll likely see most of these. If you work for a very small company, not so much. This is all of the stuff that you don't necessarily want, but that you really do need. You have "asked" your employer to pay for these items on your behalf:

- Health insurance
- Dental insurance
- Disability insurance
- 401(k) contribution
- Flexible Spending Account contribution, health savings account (HSA), etc.

Details of these benefits will be covered later in this chapter. But first, take a look at your paycheck.

Your Paycheck

There is a lot that goes in to calculating your net pay. Here's some payroll lingo:

- **Pay periods:** The length of time in which you worked and for which the employer pays your salary or wage.
- **Wage:** This is usually payment for services by the hour, the week, or occasionally the month.
- **Salary:** This is usually payment for services quoted on an annual basis.

> Net pay = gross pay – payroll taxes – federal income taxes – state income taxes – deductions.

Historically, "blue collar" workers were paid a wage (usually hourly) and "white collar" workers were paid a salary.

Typical pay periods are:

- **Biweekly:** Every two weeks, so you have 26 pay periods in a year.
- **Semimonthly:** Twice a month, usually 1st and 15th or 15th and 31st. There are 24 semimonthly pay periods per year.
- **Weekly:** Once a week, so you have 52 pay periods per year. This is typically only for hourly workers.
- **Monthly:** Once a month, so you have 12 pay periods per year.

Example: If you have a salary of $30,000 per year, and you are paid biweekly, your gross pay[5] is $1,153.85 per pay period ($30,000/26).

If you are paid hourly, your gross pay will be the number of hours worked during the pay period multiplied by your hourly rate. If you earn $15 per hour and you worked 75 hours over the two-week pay period (biweekly), your gross pay will be 15 X $75 = $1,125.

Sounds great, except from that gross pay you have to pay taxes, lots of taxes.

Taxes

Payroll Taxes

- **Social security (technically OADSI: Old-Age, Disability & Survivor's Insurance)** is an amount withheld from your gross pay which provides you a retirement benefit at age 67 (2014 retirement age) or a disability benefit if you become totally disabled. Your employer withholds 6.2 percent of your social security wage base. The maximum SS wage base is $117,000 (2014). Social security wage base is the amount of your gross pay that is subject to OASDI withholding. Certain benefits may be added to your gross pay to determine the wage base and some deductions (flexible spending contributions) reduce the wage base.

---

5 Gross Pay: Amount of compensation before any withholding or payroll deductions. Calculated as salary divided by the number of pay periods.

- **Medicare:** This is also part of social security, but this covers your future Medicare costs, which you're eligible for at age 65. The tax is 1.45 percent of your Medicare wage base (again, certain deductions may not be subject to Medicare). There is no maximum, so if you make $1 million, you pay 1.45 percent of that million to Medicare.

- **Employer match:** All employers must match the employee's OADSI and Medicare withholding.

- **Self-employment tax:** If you are self-employed, you have to essentially match your own withholding. This is called a self-employment tax, but it is exactly the same amount as the employer match. Therefore, your total OADSI tax is 12.4 percent of the first $117,000, and Medicare is 2.9 percent of your total wage base. The self-employment tax is calculated as part of your Form 1040 Federal Income Tax calculation. You use Schedule SE to actually calculate the amount of the self-employment tax liability[6].

> **FICA—Federal Insurance Contributions Act:** the legislation that created social security tax withholding. Old-timers refer to OASDI as FICA.

Income Taxes

- **Federal withholding:** The money that the employer withholds from your paycheck each pay period and sends to the U.S. Treasury on your behalf to satisfy your federal income tax liability.

- **State withholding:** The money that the employer withholds from your paycheck each pay period and sends to the state Department of Revenue on your behalf to satisfy your state income tax liability.

---

6 Tax Liability: Total amount of tax owed per the tax return. For income tax, this is the amount calculated on a tax return as the total tax based on taxable income less any tax credits. The liability gets compared to the withholding and estimated payments made during the year to determine if there is a balance due or a refund.

> **Remember that W-4?** Payroll uses that to determine how much federal and state tax to withhold from your paycheck each pay period.

Publication 15 (Circular E) has the withholding tables used to determine how much will be withheld for federal taxes (www.irs.gov). You need to know your filing status (single, married filing joint, etc.), the number of allowances from your W-4, the amount of gross pay, and the pay period in order to calculate the withholding. Go to your state's Department of Revenue website to find the withholding for your state. Or just be surprised when you get that first check, like most working adults were when they received their first check.

Rule of thumb: Assume at least 20–25 percent of your check will go to taxes (7.65 percent payroll, 1–10 percent state, 10–35 percent federal depending on your income level).

> **Did you know?**
> Alaska, Florida, Nevada, South Dakota, Texas, and Washington have no state income tax. New Hampshire and Tennessee only tax investment income, not earned income. But you know the state is getting its money somehow!

Other Deductions

Just when you thought that was all of the money coming out of your check, there's more:

- Health insurance
- Flexible spending account contribution, HSA, etc.
- Dental insurance
- Disability insurance

Insurance

Insurance coverage[7] is a big deal. Having employer-provided or employer-subsidized insurance for things like health care, disability, and life insurance can save you a lot of money.

"Just Do It" Scale

****	= Gotta do it; you are living on the edge without this
***	= Just do it
**	= This totally depends on your situation
*	= If you want to

Medical or Health Insurance****

This insurance covers the cost of medical care for you, your spouse, and your children. The premium is the amount paid to the insurance company for the insurance. The premium will be deducted from each of your paychecks to cover the cost of the insurance. The employer may or may not cover some of the cost of the premium.

How is the premium determined?

Premiums are based on many factors, but the main things that influence a self-only premium are the amount of the deductible[8] and the co-insurance[9] percentage. The deductible is the amount of money you pay for your medical care before the insurance kicks in.

A lower deductible = a higher premium

---

7 Coverage: Services that the insurance pays for.

8 Deductible: Amount paid by the insured in medical costs before the health plan pays the remainder of costs.

9 Co-insurance: Requires that the policy holder and the insurance company split the cost of certain expenses which are covered under the insurance. For example, a common co-insurance for medical policies is 80/20 meaning that the insurance company pays 80 percent of the cost of the medical bill (after the deductible has been met) and the policy holder pays 20 percent.

Example: Your deductible is $500. You go to the "doc in a box" because you have the flu. The total cost of your visit is $170. You have to pay that $170 yourself, and it's applied to your deductible. You will have to pay another $330 dollars yourself before your insurance company will begin to pay on your behalf.

Once you meet your deductible, the co-insurance determines how much of the next dollar of cost the insurance company pays. Commonly, it will be 80 percent/20 percent meaning that the company will pay 80 percent of the cost, and you will pay 20 percent once you have met the deductible.

Different services may have different co-insurance percentages. Your policy might cover 90 percent of the hospital cost, and 80 percent of the cost of the doctors. You have to read the plan benefits to know the co-insurance as well as the exclusions[10].

The good news is that the co-insurance does have a maximum amount that you will have to pay in the event of a big claim[11]. This maximum is usually quoted as "80 percent/20 percent with a stop loss of $5,000." The stop loss is the maximum amount that the insured (you) will have co-insurance applied against.

Example: You have a plan with $1,000 deductible, co-insurance at 80/20, and a stop loss of $20,000.

That means during the plan year, you pay 100% of the first $1,000 in claims. For the next $19,000, you will pay 20% or $3,800. Everything above $20,000 is paid by the insurance company.

In this example, if you have a serious, expensive health issue, the most you will pay is $4,800 ($1,000 of deductible and $3,800 on the co-

---

10 Exclusions: A type of service not covered by the insurance contract. For example, acupuncture or other alternative treatments may not be covered.

11 Claim: Formal request by a policy holder for payment of incurred expenses which are covered under the terms of the insurance policy.

insurance.). This is also called the out-of-pocket maximum. It lets you know how much you are on the hook for.

Here's a bad news alert: At the start of the next plan year, you are back to $0. So, if you get sick or injured, do it early in the plan year. Note: The plan year is the 12-month period used to determine if you have met your deductible or other plan thresholds. For most plans this will be a calendar year, but it does not have to be.

Co-pay[12] is another way that plans may provide coverage. You pay a flat fee every time you go to a doctor in the plan network[13], usually about $20 to $25. Co-pays may relate to preventative care; the insurance company wants well people to maintain their health, give their kids immunizations, get routine check-ups, etc. A low co-pay is an incentive for you to take care of yourself and catch little problems before they become big (expensive) problems.

Maximum out-of-pocket is an amount that is defined for each option within the plan that will tell you the maximum you will pay in one year if the worst happens. This is an important number to know. It is a combination of the deductible plus the co-insurance maximum.

Exclusions

It is critical to know what your insurance won't pay for. Sometimes mental health providers are excluded or limited. Rehab might also be excluded (or limited). Some policies exclude maternity, which is fine if you are a guy, but not so much for 20-something females.

---

12 Co-pay: In health insurance, this is a defined amount that the policy holder will pay when visiting a service provider. A common co-pay for a doctor visit may be $20 to $25. The policy holder pays that at the time of the visit and the doctor bills the insurance company for the balance of the cost.

13 Network: Doctors and medical facilities that the insurance company has contracted with to provide services at set rates.

Types of Health Plans

The landscape of health care and health insurance is changing as a result of the Affordable Care Act, also known as "Obamacare." Much of that has not been implemented as of this writing, so take this information as a history lesson and use the information to carefully review current health insurance offerings. Check the website www.graduatesguidetomoney.com for updates.

- **HMO:** A health maintenance organization (HMO) has doctors on staff to treat the plan members. Kaiser Permanente is the most well-known.

The Good
<ul><li>Your preventative care is very inexpensive or free.</li><li>Frequently, you just pay a co-pay (a set fee per visit) every time you visit the doctor, regardless of the type of doctor you see.</li><li>If you have a chronic or long-term condition, coordination of your care may be a huge benefit.</li></ul>
The Bad
You have to see an HMO doctor/go to an HMO facility,* or there is no coverage. <ul><li>HMOs require you to work through your Primary Care Physician (PCP) in order to see any type of specialist.</li><li>Depending on where you live, it might be hard/inconvenient to find HMO facilities.</li></ul>*Except in a life-threatening situation.
The Ugly
<ul><li>Premiums tend to be a lot higher as compared to other plans.</li></ul>

- **PPO:** Preferred Provider Organizations (PPO) have contracted with a network of physicians, hospitals, and labs to provide services to members at pre-arranged rates. They are similar to HMOs in that you have to go to a doctor within the network to get the discounted rate. PPOs will provide coverage to out-of-network[14] patients, but at a higher cost, whereas HMOs won't cover the cost at all.

The Good
▪ The network is usually pretty extensive. ▪ The contractual rates are significantly less than you would pay as an uninsured patient. ▪ You don't need a referral to specialists (unless the specialist or specialty service requires it). ▪ There are usually a lot of deductible choices, so you can manage the premium cost by adjusting the deductible.
The Bad
▪ They are structured under the "deductible, co-pay" model so you will pay out-of-pocket at every doctor visit until you meet your deductible.
The Ugly
▪ There is a pretty steep penalty for using an out-of-network doctor or facility.

▪ **POS:** A point-of-service plan is another name for a PPO. These plans are called point-of-service because you decide at the time you need a doctor, what kind of doctor to see (generalist or specialist) and whether to stay in-network or to go out-of-network.

---

14 Out-of-Network: In health insurance, the insurance company will define a network of medical service providers that the policy holder may use and be considered "in network" and thus pay a lower fee. The insurance company has contracts with the providers which defines the costs. Any service provider not defined as "in network" is out-of-network. There are typically higher charges when out-of-network providers are used (or the cost may not be covered at all or may be subject to a higher deductible).

- **HDHP:** A high deductible health plan is a PPO plan with an unusually high deductible. The plan qualifies the plan holder to use an HSA in conjunction with the plan. An HSA lets you deposit money into a savings account to pay for medical or dental expenses in the future. Go to www.irs.gov and search for Publication 969: Health Savings Accounts and Other Tax-Favored Health Plans to get details.

The Good
▪ You get to deduct on your tax return the money you put into this account every year, up to $3,300 for self-only coverage and $6,550 for family coverage (2014).
▪ The interest you earn on the money in the account is not subject to any taxes.
▪ You can let the money accumulate over your whole life if you want to with no penalty and no tax.
▪ You can use the money to pay any qualified medical or dental expenses for you or your dependents[15].
▪ The premiums on qualifying health plans are usually lower than with traditional health plans.
The Bad
▪ To qualify to set up this type of account, you must have a special health plan called a High Deductible Health Plan (HDHP).
▪ The deductible must be at least $1,250 for an individual or $2,500 for a family, but not more than $6,350 and $12,700 (2014).
▪ Not every employer offers this type of plan.

---

15 Dependent: A person the taxpayer supports who meets the tax code definition of a dependent. The taxpayer claims an exemption on his or her tax return for each dependent, which helps reduce taxable income.

The Ugly
• You can't withdraw the money unless you have qualified medical or dental expenses. If you do withdraw money for other things, you will pay federal and state taxes on the amount withdrawn, and you will pay a 20 percent penalty (that's on top of the income tax due).

- **Preferred Choice HDHP with HSA:** If you are healthy, you probably won't meet your deductible under a "normal" plan anyway, so why not set a really high deductible and get the lower premium? This option allows you to have lower premiums than other options. You also have the ability to save to an HSA account to accumulate a fund for the future, and to deduct the HSA savings even if you don't itemize on your tax return. You can withdraw money for qualifying medical expenses years after you actually incur the expense (keep your receipts for every medical cost you paid with non-HSA dollars).

This option covers 100 percent of your expenses over your deductible amount, so you are insuring for a big, bad event. When you have the HSA funded up to the amount of your deductible, you know you have your worst case scenario 100 percent covered. All of this helps you become a more informed, more responsible consumer of medical services.

How do you determine which option is right for you?

Insurance is all about giving your risk to someone else. Who will pay if something big, bad, and ugly happens? A horrendous accident or life-changing diagnosis can ruin you financially if you don't have insurance. On the other hand, you can pay a lot of premiums for a long time and never have any claims. How's that crystal ball working?

Make sure you are 100 percent insured on the really big stuff, but take on all of the risk for the little stuff. What's little? That depends on you and your financial situation. What is the most that could come out of your budget/savings if you had unusually high medical expenses: $1,000? $2,000?

The good news is that doctors and hospitals are used to working with people who need time to pay, so they usually will provide no-interest financing for fees that you can't pay all at once.

How much does it cost? (2014 generalization)

- A visit to a family physician or "generalist" is $100.
- A "doc in a box" is $80.
- A complete physical $400.
- "Lab" costs for basic stuff is $50.

Analyze the choices

Amount of your expected doctor visits annually   _____

Amount of your expected prescription costs annually   _____

Total expected medical costs   _____

Do you think you could afford to pay 100 percent of that yourself out of your monthly salary or savings? If you could, then you need to insure for "the big stuff" and pay for your normal medical costs yourself. You want to pay the minimum amount of premiums, and still be 100 percent covered for all costs over $X. How much is X? Expect your max out-of-pocket cost on most plans to be in the $5,000 to $20,000 range. You have to look at the plans and compare the deductibles, co-insurance (70/30, 80/20, sometimes 90/10), stop loss, maximum out-of-pocket amounts, coverages, and exclusions.

If you have a chronic condition that requires regular doctor visits, prescription drugs, or other treatments, you should identify the annual cost of all that under the various plans. Be sure to include the premium cost when comparing the plans.

Here is a table for your use in comparing the various choices you have. (See Appendix for Health Insurance Comparison Worksheet.)

	Option 1	Option 2	Option 3
Annual Premium			
Annual Deductible			
Co-Insurance Percentage			
Co-Insurance Limit			
Max Out-of-Pocket Cost			
Is what I need covered?			
Any exclusions that will impact me?			
Is it HSA qualified?			

Fill in the details for each of the plan options. Your last two rows will be "Best case cost" and "Worst case cost."

Best case cost = annual premium + amount of expected medical costs (considering deductible and co-insurance)

Worst case cost = annual premium + maximum out-of-pocket cost

Compare the options

- Can you rule out an option based on coverages or exclusions?
- Which option has the lowest best case total cost?
- Which option has the lowest worst case total cost?
- For the plans with the lowest cost, are your current doctors in the plan network?
- Are there plenty of network doctors and facilities in your area?
- Does anything concern you about the lowest cost option?

> If you have any questions about how the plan works, ask your human resources department. These folks are paid to know this stuff. If they can't answer your question, they can put you in touch with someone who can.

This process seems kind of complicated, but if you actually fill out the table, your best option will become clear. This is your money and your health; don't just check a box.

Flexible Spending Accounts (Flex Plans)**

These plans let you withhold money from your paycheck before taxes are withheld in order to pay for medical or childcare expenses.

The Good
▪ You are able to pay for medical and childcare expenses with pre-tax dollars. That saves you not only federal and state taxes but also payroll taxes. Even in the lowest tax bracket, the savings can be at over 17 percent just in payroll and federal taxes.
The Bad
▪ You have to be able to accurately estimate the amount you need in each category (medical or childcare) at the beginning of the plan year.
▪ For plan years after 2012, the IRS imposed a limit on the maximum amount you can contribute to these plans ($2,000 for medical and $5,000 for dependent care).
The Ugly
▪ If you don't use all of the money you withheld for these expenses, you lose it at the end of the plan year.
▪ Like everything IRS, there are lots of rules and regulations, so read and understand all the details.
See IRS publication 969 at www.irs.gov for details.

Dental****

This insurance covers the cost of ... yes, going to the dentist. Almost all dental plans use the model of very low cost or free check-ups and pretty high co-insurance (or set fee) on anything corrective, such as fillings, crowns, root canals, etc. Some plans may have a deductible, but that is not common.

You must have dental insurance. It's not expensive, and it's not nearly as complicated as health insurance. You can use the same chart to compare the various options. Your biggest consideration is determining which dentists are in the plan's network, are conveniently located near your workplace, and have extended hours of operation.

Disability****, Life**, and Accidental Death*

Chapter 7 provides more information about disability and other types of insurance. Here is a general overview of what you need to know about these insurance options when you begin working.

> According to the U.S. Census Bureau, you have a one in five chance of becoming disabled.

Disability Insurance

This coverage will replace your monthly income if you become disabled and cannot work. You might be thinking, "That will never happen to me." Nobody thinks they will get plowed over by a truck or stricken by a debilitating disease, but it happens every day. In your 20s and 30s, you are more likely to be disabled than to die, so this insurance is essential. You want the maximum percentage of your income (usually 67 percent).

The typical disability timeline is:

PTO – Sick Leave (2-4 weeks) (defined by employer)
<ul><li>Use your sick days (commonly referred to as PTO (Personal Time Off) up to the max provided by your employer.</li><li>Big companies may give you four weeks of PTO as a new employee, which includes your vacation and activities you need to handle during work hours.</li></ul>
Short-Term Disability (up to 90 days)
<ul><li>Once your PTO runs out, you tap into your short-term disability policy.</li><li>This policy will typically pay 67 percent of your salary for the period defined in the policy (12 weeks is common) if you cannot work due to a medical condition, whether accident or injury.</li><li>Short-term disability can be a company provided benefit, but don't assume that it is.</li><li>If it's not company provided, buy the insurance unless you have enough savings to cover 12 weeks of living expenses without pay.</li></ul>
Long-Term Disability
<ul><li>This policy picks up when your short-term disability coverage lapses.</li><li>The waiting period is the length of time you have to wait before your benefit starts. Both ST and LT disability can have waiting periods. The waiting period is typically at least 90 days for LTD.</li><li>The policy will pay the benefit (as defined in the policy: 67 percent of salary if you chose that) for the period of time defined in the policy. Ideally, this will be until age 67, but could be only one to two years.</li></ul>

Paying premiums with "post-tax dollars"

- Your employer will take out all of your taxes and then subtract your disability premium.
- If you were ever disabled and had to receive a benefit check, it would be income tax-free.
- If you are only able to get 67 percent of your salary, you definitely want it to be tax-free.

This is the way to go!

Paying premiums with "pre-tax dollars"

- Your employer will take out your disability premium and then calculate the amount of taxes based on the net.
- If you were ever disabled and had to receive a benefit check, it would be taxable income.

If you are getting 67 percent of your salary and then have to pay tax out of it, that could hurt. Ouch!

If you are self-employed, you will have to make a lot more decisions about your coverage than if you are an employee with a group policy. If you don't want to be dependent on someone else financially should you become disabled, disability insurance is a must-have. Talk to a knowledgeable insurance agent who specializes in disability policies and make sure you understand the impact of each option.

Life Insurance

This type of policy pays a beneficiary if you die. It is totally for the benefit of the family you leave behind. Often, larger companies will provide a benefit equal to at least your salary as an employee benefit (meaning it's free to you). If you want more coverage, you can pay the additional premium cost.

If you are:

Single, no kids
• 1x salary is probably sufficient to cover your final expenses (funeral, burial, etc. ~$15,000).
• Any excess goes to pay your debts.
• Anything remaining goes to your beneficiaries.
Married, no kids
• Need ~$15,000 to cover final expenses.
• Should get enough benefit to pay off all debts.
• Add in amount of nest egg that you would want your spouse to have. Plan on at least one year of your spouse's salary.
• You may max out of what you can get through your employer. If so, review Chapter 7 for more about buying life insurance.
Married with kids
• Complete the insurance needs analysis in Chapter 7.
• Group life is usually about as inexpensive as life insurance gets.
• The downside: it's typically not portable, meaning, if you quit, you can't take it with you.

Beneficiaries: Who Gets the Money?

- **Primary beneficiary:** The person (or people) who will receive your life insurance benefit if you die and they are still living. There is no limit to the number of beneficiaries you can designate. The beneficiary can also be an entity (like a trust), a charity, or a company.
  - **Per stirpes:** If you identify a beneficiary with a per stirpes designation, that means if that beneficiary is deceased at the time you die, that person's share will go to any of his or her lineal descendants (children, grandchildren, great-grand-children).

- **Per capita:** If you identify a beneficiary with a per capita designation, that means if that beneficiary is deceased at the time you die, that person's share will be split evenly among your other primary beneficiaries.
- **Contingent beneficiary:** The person (or people) who will receive your benefit if you die and the primary beneficiaries are all deceased, or they disclaim (refuse) the benefit. These beneficiaries get nothing unless all of the primary beneficiaries are deceased or disclaim (and if you designated per stirpes, if they had no children or those children are also deceased).

Accidental Death and Dismemberment (AD&D)*

This policy pays extra if you die in an accident, and it pays a pre-established benefit if you are dismembered (lose a limb). Sometimes this is a rider[16] (add-on) to the life insurance policy. If it's free, get it.

Stock Plans

401(k) Plan****

Now we're getting to the good stuff! Free money!! 401(k) plans are retirement plans so there are specific rules related to these plans:

- Money is withheld from your paycheck before income taxes are calculated so you do not pay income tax on money deposited to these accounts.
- There is an annual limit to how much you contribute: $17,500 in 2014.

---

16 Rider: Add-on item on an insurance contract. A rider for a homeowner's or renter's policy might be high-dollar items like jewelry or electronics. There is typically an add-on cost to having a rider. Riders can also cover added services such as cost-of-living adjustments on a long-term care policy or renewability provisions on a disability policy.

- You cannot withdraw money from the account until you are 59 1/2, disabled, or you die (your beneficiary would take the withdrawal). There are a few other unique situations but basically think of this money as "untouchable" until you retire.
- If you do take money out, you will pay federal and state income taxes as well as pay a 10 percent penalty.
- Employers will usually provide some kind of match often based on a percentage of what the employee contributes.
  - They might say, "the company will match 50 percent of the employee contribution up to 4 percent of salary."
    - That means that you must contribute 8 percent of your annual salary in order to get the maximum company match.
  - Or it might be, "the company will match 100 percent of the employee's contribution up to a maximum of 3 percent of salary."
    - In that case, you would need to contribute 3 percent of your salary to get the full match.
  - Definitely contribute enough to get 100 percent of the match. This is free money! If it is at all possible, contribute enough to "fully fund" the 401(k) up to the legal limit ($17,500 for 2014).
  - To calculate that percentage, divide the limit ($17,500) by your salary.
  - Don't be surprised if your company match comes in the form of company stock (if you work for a public company meaning one that trades on a stock exchange).
- Some plans may have a vesting[17] provision.

---

17 Vesting: Provision in a benefit plan that requires the employee to stay employed with the company for some period of time (the vesting period) in order to earn the benefit.

- For example, "the employer contribution will vest at 25 percent per year."
  - This means that on your one-year anniversary, you will have earned 25 percent of what the company matched in your 401(k).
  - You are always 100 percent vested in your contribution from day one.
  - After four years, you will be 100 percent vested so everything that the company has matched and will match in the future is yours if you quit.
  - There could be longer or shorter vesting periods or no vesting provision at all. Read, read, read the details . . . or ask HR!
- The plan will list various mutual funds that you can choose to invest in. See Chapter 8: "Saving and Investing" for details on how to make your selection of investments.

Whew! You thought getting the job was the hard part. There is definitely a lot to the payroll and benefits part of life, but at the end of the paper trail, you do get a paycheck, a smaller one than you thought, but a paycheck nonetheless. Now that you have the cash, check out the next chapter because you're going to start spending it.

CHAPTER 3

Paying the Bills:
So You're Not Rich

In this chapter:

- What Are the Big Money Rocks?
- Creating a Cash Flow Plan
- Using Credit Cards
- Tips For Getting To Financial Independence

Most people rebel against a budget. "How restrictive!" "How confining!" "It's like money jail!" Most people are actually dead wrong. "How freeing!" Developing a budget is nothing more than deciding, in a cool, clear way, what your most important money priorities are.

It's easy to be the queen of "It's only five bucks." You could "It's only five bucks" your way to a $300 basket at Target in a heartbeat with this mindset. You could five or ten-buck your way to $500 at Amazon in a week. This is the absolute worst money mindset there is. You could eat up a paycheck on NOTHING, five bucks at a time, literally robbing yourself of the things you truly want by dribbling away money on things you actually didn't need or care much about and deluding yourself that small amounts don't matter.

Here's the truest get-rich secret on the planet: small amounts add up to big amounts. This is a get rich slow method that will benefit you if you're the "It's only five bucks" kind of person. Five bucks adds up whether you spend it or save it consistently over time. Why is it so easy to put that five bucks in the shopping cart, but so hard to put it in the savings account? Maybe because you haven't adopted the Ben Franklin mindset: "A penny saved is a penny earned." That's the first important rule of getting rich.

The second important rule is, "Put the big rocks in first." Here's the big rock story. This story shows up on a lot of websites. One of them credited it to Stephen Covey, author of *The Seven Habits of Highly Effective People:*

> A college professor pulls out a Mason jar one day in front of his class. He then lays a pile of good sized rocks next to it. He begins to place the big rocks into the jar. When no more rocks will fit in, he asks the class, "Is the jar full?" They reply, "Yes."
>
> He then pulls out some gravel and pours the gravel into the jar, shaking it so it can settle in between the big rocks. Again he asks, "Is the jar full?" and again they reply, "Yes."
>
> He then pulls out some pea gravel and pours that into the jar shaking it to allow the pea gravel to settle. By this time, the class tentatively replies that the jar is probably not full yet.
>
> He repeats the process with sand and then with water. "What is the moral of the story?" he asks.
>
> "You can always add a little bit more," tries one student.
>
> "Not exactly." He then pulls out another Mason jar and fills it with water. "Is this jar full?" he asks.
>
> "Yes," they reply.
>
> "I agree," he says. "The water represents all of the little things in life that can fill up an hour or a day or a week. The big rocks are the most important things in your life. If you do not put the big rocks into the jar first, you will never fit them in."

What Are the Big Money Rocks?

Only you know the answer to that question for you. It is important to define your big rocks when it comes to your money so you can create a money plan around those highest priorities. Here are some thoughts:

Charity

Most people with a spiritual mindset will tell you that charity should come off the top.

Financial Security

- **Short-term:** Emergency fund, liquidity fund, rainy day money; call it what you will, but you need a ready source of cash if life hands you lemons (as in your car is a lemon) or you get down-sized or capsized by your employer. Experts say three to six months of expenses. I say, what is the amount that makes you feel safe? My number is pretty high and when my fund starts getting low, I feel like I can't breathe when I think about it. I like breathing so I try to keep cash at a level that makes me breathe easy.

- **Long-term:** Retirement is for grandpa but financial independence is for YOU.

Retirement	Financial Independence
- Seems very far away (someday-land, right up there with "tomorrow" . . . never happens). - Old people retire ("I'm never going to be that old!").	- Something you can get to at 30, 40, 50. - Do whatever you want without concern about a paycheck. Wouldn't it be great to not have to work at age 30 because you have enough money to support yourself until age 100?

Lifestyle

Lifestyle is the way you live, the stuff you need, the stuff you like, the places you enjoy going, plus all of the other stuff that amounts to the style of your life. Look at it this way:

- **Necessary expenses.** This includes food, rent, utilities, gas, and insurance: all of the not fun parts of life that must be paid just to survive. Lifestyle also includes your car (new or used, luxury or economy, gas guzzler, or alternative energy?), your living space (rent or own, apartment or house, roommates or single-living, city or suburbs?), your food (eat out or cook in, raw or pre-made, junky or healthy?), and your clothing (formal or casual, new or lightly used, designer or basic?).

- **Accumulation.** This is the stuff of life. How important is it to you to load up on stuff like entertainment, travel, self-care, and experiences? This includes concerts, movies, weekend getaways, extended vacations, spa days, tattoos, piercings, snowboarding, surfing, and any number of related activities and experiences. How big are these rocks in your jar?

Carefully think through these areas of your life and decide what's most important to you, then make a plan to put your money where your heart is.

Creating a Cash Flow Plan

A cash flow plan, also known as a budget, is a road map to help keep you on track to achieve your financial goals. There are a lot of thoughts on budgets. Google "budgeting tips" and you get over 47 million hits. That's a lot of thoughts! Here are some common approaches:

- **Ratios.** Lenders use ratios which say that your housing cost should be less than 30 percent of your income, and your total debt load should be less than 43 percent of your income. You can create a spending plan based on these ratios to calculate how much rent you can afford given your other debts.

- **Budget categories.** In this approach, break down your spending into categories like housing, food, personal care, etc. Software like Quicken or websites like mint.com will automate this process by downloading transactions from your bank and credit cards and categorizing the most common things like gas, groceries, clothing, etc.

- **Savings.** Plan for your savings first (at 10 percent to 20 percent of your income, ideally) and then look at what remains to cover your living expenses and consumer debt.

- **Fixed expenses versus variable expenses.** Examine your spending by fixed (the monthly amount doesn't change: rent, car payment, etc.) versus variable (credit cards, utilities).

- **Needs versus wants.** In this approach, break down your spending into what you must pay (rent, utilities, loans) versus what you want to buy.

At its most basic, your spending plan compares the money you have coming in each month to what you expect your monthly expenses to be.

Take a simple "big picture" approach to figure out what you have available for spending (See example cash flow plan to get the visual). Open up an Excel file (or grab paper and pencil):

- In the first column, write out the days of the month one through 31 (you may need a couple of lines for the first). The next columns will be "description," "payment amount," and "running cash balance."

- Write in your net pay next to the date you get paid (if you are paid bi-weekly, it will shift each month so put it in the 1st and 15th to give you a sense of your monthly cash flow) and then carry that amount over to the running cash balance column.

- Write in your savings right after your paycheck since you are, of course, paying yourself first, and update the running cash balance to reflect the money out.

- Write in each bill and loan payment you have to pay next to the date it is due. Rent or mortgage is usually due on the first so you may need a couple of lines for that date. Make sure you cover everything you have to pay. Use an estimate for variable expenses like utilities and credit cards.

- Include cash withdrawals at your weekly average.
- Include an "other" line item because life happens and it usually costs. Plan to build up a cushion each month and then be thankful if you don't have to dip into it.
- Continue to update the running cash balance.

Example Cash Flow Plan:

Day	Description (who you pay)	Payment amount	Running cash balance
1	Paycheck	1100	1100
1	To savings	(110)	990
1	Rent	(500)	490
2	Car insurance	(200)	290
3	Cash	(50)	240
4	Car payment	(250)	(10)
10	Visa (groceries and gas)	(300)	(310)
11	Cash	(50)	(360)
12	Cell phone	(45)	(405)
15	Paycheck	1100	695
15	To savings	(110)	585

> Timing looks to be a problem here. Even though it all works out in the end, you may want to see if you can adjust some due dates to even out the cash out or you have to have some cushion in your checking account.

Analyze the results:

- Do you project that you will have positive cash flow (more cash in than out) for the month?
- Is there any time during the month when your daily balance goes negative? If so, you need to build up reserves to ensure that you don't actually go negative.
- Do you have some wiggle room or are you down to the penny?
- Regardless of your answers, look for ways to trim back so you can pay down debt more quickly or save for a "big rock" item.

- Track your actual balance versus this projection each month. You can do this low-tech with a notebook and pencil or you can use one of the many electronic tools available.

The bottom line is that you have to find some way to know what money is committed (bills you must pay) and what money is discretionary (available for spending).

Other Tools

There are a number of software packages you can use which help with organizing and tracking your financial life. Here are a few:

- Quicken (or Microsoft Money). Made by Intuit (maker of TurboTax and QuickBooks), this software resides on your computer's hard drive and allows you to do an online backup for a fee. This software is intuitive, easy to use, and has a lot of tutorials. However, the downside is that it resides on your hard drive, so you have to access your computer to get to it. The good news is that you can password protect it. Visit www.quicken.intuit.com for a list of features.

- Mint.com (owned by Intuit) is an online program for tracking spending and net worth.
- QuickBooks (Intuit) is software for small businesses. If you have a small business, QuickBooks is easy to use and very powerful for the price.

Using Credit Cards

Credit cards are a great tool, and probably a must-have in today's world. They help you build credit and can provide for fast relief in an emergency if you haven't built up enough in your emergency savings.

Unfortunately, people can get out of control with credit cards, often because using them doesn't seem like spending real money. Small amounts accumulate quickly and before you know it, the balance is high. If you don't pay off the balance each month, the interest charges get crazy expensive quickly. It's easy to say you'll worry about it later, but worry doesn't make the payment. Unless you set up balance alerts, it's hard to keep up with how much you've charged.

To get started on the right foot with using credit cards, only charge "must have" items like gas, food, or dry cleaning. You've already budgeted for these items, so you know you'll be able to pay the total balance at the end of the month. Avoid the temptation to buy items you probably shouldn't buy simply because you don't have the cash in hand.

Use cash—real dollar bills—to buy "want" items. Getting a new TV? Go to the bank and pull out the cash for that purchase. This practice forces you to consider the cost of tax and delivery fees as part of the price, and there is no justifying something more expensive because "it's only $X more." You don't have $X more! Plus, holding that much money in your hand will make you think carefully about buying that TV. This approach will also cut down on emotional, heat-of-the-moment purchases. Having to go get cash takes you out of the situation for long enough to let the emotion of the moment fade.

Tips For Getting To Financial Independence

- Pay yourself first.
- Automate the process.
- "Five buck" your way to wealth.
- Create a system to keep your big rock items top of mind.
- Think long and hard before you buy a new car; it drops in value the minute you drive off the car lot. Used is a much better deal, and driving the car you have is usually even better.
- Use the envelope system. Identify how much you spend on a certain category (like eating out or entertainment) and put cash in the envelope each pay period. When the envelope is empty, you're done spending.
- Create your own tracking and reward system and make a game out of living cheap.

Life is much less stressful when you don't have to worry about money all the time. Create a plan for yourself before you commit to debt or a big lifestyle, and you will feel in control of your financial life. Being secure in the knowledge that you are spending your money according to the things that are most important to you in the long run is worth any sacrifice you make.

CHAPTER 4

Net Worth

In this chapter:

- What Is Net Worth?
- Tips For Increasing Your Net Worth
- Action Plan For Your Net Worth

What Is Net Worth?

Assets – Liabilities (Debts) = Net Worth

Net worth[18] is a snapshot of where you are financially at any point in time and is a measure of financial security. Tracking your net worth over time can be very revealing and motivating.

> Your net worth helps you answer the questions,
> - "Where am I financially?"
> - "Am I going in the right direction (over time)?"

Certain software will track your net worth when you put in all of your assets and debts. If you don't use a software program, here is a simple way to set up your net worth schedule.

---

18 Net worth: Total assets minus total liabilities. It is a measure of how financially secure a person is.

Assets	Value	Liabilities (Debts)	Balance	Net
Liquid Assets:		Credit cards:		
Checking account	1,000	Visa	4,000	
Savings account	5,000	Mastercard	1,000	
Emergency Fund	10,000	American Express		
Goals account	500	Store card	2,000	
		Store card		
Total Liquid Assets	16,500	**Total credit cards**	7,000	9,500
Financial Independence:				
IRA	-	Student loans	10,000	
Roth IRA	1,000	Student loans	3,000	
401k	4,000	Student loans	8,000	
Investment account	-			
Total Financial Independence	5,000	**Total student loans**	21,000	(16,000)
Other Assets:				
Car	10,000	Car loan	5,000	
House	200,000	Mortgage loan	175,000	
Total Other Assets	210,000	**Total loans**	180,000	30,000
Total Assets	231,500	**Total Liabilities**	208,000	23,500

Assets: Having "liquid" assets means you can pay your bills. Liquid assets are cash or are easily converted to cash, and are available to meet cash flow needs. It is a big transition to go from having no financial responsibility to being totally responsible for paying your way. If you paid your own way through college, you know how true this is. And you probably also know how painful it is when you run out of money before you run out of month. Having a reserve of cash on hand helps during those lean times.

Other assets, like your TV, clothes, and even your car lose value over time. Your car belongs on your net worth statement (also called a balance sheet) only if it has a loan attached to it, because it is dropping in value every day. If it has a loan, then you want to add it to be able to compare the asset and the loan.

If you have some kind of collection or other assets, which could appreciate in value, you can add them.

Asset value includes the following:

- **Bank, investment, financial independence accounts:** The value of the account will technically be market value, especially if you have stocks, bonds, or mutual funds in the account, as the custodian will value the account based on the market price for that day.

- **Car, house, and the like:** Value these items at the price you originally paid for them or try to determine the market value. However, market value isn't really a value until you have someone who is willing to write you a check for the item.

Liabilities or debts: The creditor will tell you exactly how much you owe. Liabilities are everything from your monthly cell phone bill or rent payment, which are recurring payments, to student loan payments to credit cards. The bottom line is that you got something and you have to pay for it after the fact.

Net Worth: Assets – Liabilities

- Your net worth may be negative, especially if you came out of college with student loans. This simply means that you haven't converted your earnings potential into dollars yet.

- Your net worth is as of a single point in time which is great because that means you can change it tomorrow.

- Your net worth is all about the journey. The important thing is planning for it to go up over time and then implementing that plan.

   Example: Mary has a net worth of $23,500 according to the sample net worth schedule. If Mary is 23, that's fantastic! If Mary is 60, maybe not so great as Mary's working years (accumulation years) are dwindling. Everything is relative, and net worth is no different. Sure, a high net worth gives you more options than a low net worth, but it is all about how you want to live your life and what is most important to you.

Regardless of your "magic number" for net worth, you should:

- Know your net worth now;

- Set goals about where you want your net worth to be over time; and

- Track your progress toward your net worth goal.

Net worth versus annual salary: This is a reflection of how many "years" of work you have saved. If Mary's salary is $20,000 per year, her net worth represents a little over one year's worth of work. It also means, in theory, that she could quit her job and live for one year on her assets. This is a big picture way of estimating your level of financial independence. How many years could you live on your current net worth?

Liquid assets to credit cards: The goal is not to have any credit card debt as you should strive to pay off the balance in full each month. If you aren't quite there yet, compare the two figures. Here, Mary has about $2.35 dollars of assets available to pay every dollar of credit card debt. So, she could pay off all of her credit cards right now. That's a nice spot to be in. Should she? That depends. These strategies are covered in the next chapter.

Financial independence assets versus student loan debt: The comparison here is about seeing if you have "covered" your college education investment yet by generating enough financial independence savings to cover your outstanding student loan debt. Going to college is most definitely an investment and a pretty steep investment in many cases. Maybe you were fortunate to have someone who paid for your education and you have no debt. Someone invested in you or you were savvy enough and smart enough to get your education through scholarships or by working and paying as you went. If you do have some debt from college expenses, it may make you feel better knowing that your earning power is creating financial independence for yourself. Here, Mary hasn't quite gotten the financial independence fund to exceed the remaining student loan debt, but it is a great motivator to watch this ratio drop as she adds money to her 401(k) while she pays down the student loan debt.

Other assets versus the related debt: This will show you how much equity is in your house or car. Mary bought her car for $10,000 and has a $5,000 loan on it, so her equity is theoretically $5,000. If she could sell the car for $10,000, that would be true. If she could only sell the car for $8,000, then the real equity is only $3,000 rather than $5,000. The relationship tends to hold better on a house than a car because a house generally does not decrease in value over time (although it definitely can).

Tips For Increasing Net Worth

- Don't add new debt!
- Don't add new debt!
- Don't add new debt! Think this is critical?
  - Every dollar of new debt decreases your net worth by $1.
  - Even if you buy an investment asset using debt, like a $50,000 piece of land, you still have no change to net worth because you added a $50,000 asset and a $50,000 liability. The total assets increase and so do the liabilities.
- Pay off debt out of your incoming cash flow in order to increase your net worth.
  - Using assets to pay off debt doesn't change your net worth.

Assets – liabilities = net worth

231,500	– 208,000	= 23,500
(7,000)	(7,000)	use 7,000 of savings to pay off credit cards
224,500	– 201,000	= 23,500

Both assets and liabilities are reduced by the same amount, so net worth stays the same.

Increase your net worth by adding to savings out of incoming cash flow. Think of the power of adding money to savings and paying down debt at the same time. You are both increasing assets and decreasing debt.

Action Plan For Your Net Worth

1. Calculate your net worth to determine the best way to track it going forward. How will you track it? How often will you track it?

2. Define clearly what you want your net worth to be and by when. This is the big hairy crazy goal. It will definitely seem terrifying and not very achievable. Not "debt free by tomorrow," but maybe "debt free in a year." Not "$1 million in the bank tomorrow," but maybe "$1 million in the bank by next year."

3. Complete this:

   - I want my net worth to be _____ by _____ (make this a goal within the next one to two years).

   - I want my net worth to be _____ by _____ (make this a goal within the next five years).

   - I want my net worth to be _____ by _____ (make this a goal within the next ten years).

4. Learn this and live it if you want to see your net worth grow: "Don't sacrifice what you want **most** for what you want **now**."

   - Sacrifice is the ultimate "must do" in order to grow net worth.

   - You have to be willing to give up today's shiny bauble in order to save money or pay off debt.

   - Are you willing to sacrifice what you want in this moment to get where you want to be?

   - What will you sacrifice and what won't you sacrifice?

5. Look at your cash flow plan from Chapter 3. Where can you eliminate some spending to make room for more net worth increasing?

6. If net worth is not the motivating factor for you, then try setting goals around debt. You can adjust item 2 to reflect your debt reduction goals.

Having a high net worth may not be a top priority for you, or even a priority at all, but net worth helps you feel secure and confident that you can take care of yourself in good times and in bad. Having no money limits your choices and your options. Two hundred years ago, having a gun, some tools, and a horse made you secure. Those markers of security have been traded for net worth, credit capacity, and earning potential.

Some say that money is power, but money is also freedom: freedom to choose what you want to do and when you want to do it, freedom to support the causes that are important to you with time, talent, or treasure, and freedom from being dependent on someone else to pay your way. Only you can decide what level of freedom is important to you and what you are willing to give up in order to get there.

Think about what kind of financial life you want and what level of net worth would create freedom and peace of mind for you. You have the power to make that vision a reality, but only if you make thoughtful, conscious decisions, set some goals, and actively pursue them.

CHAPTER 5

Debt

In this chapter:

- Interest
- Your Credit Score
- Credit Cards, Rates, and Minimum Payments
- How Is Your Debt Situation?

I owe, I owe, it's off to work I go. Debt is the great American burden. It may be a necessary part of modern life, but do not take it lightly. Nothing enslaves you faster than debt, so think carefully before you incur any and then work like the dickens to pay it off as fast as you can.

Interest

Borrowing money isn't free. Whoever lends you the money has plenty of other things to do with it, so if you want to rent it for some period of time, you have to pay for the use of it. This rent is called interest and is quoted as a percentage of the outstanding loan for one year. The calculation of interest is:

Interest (I) = Principal (P) x Rate (R) x Time (T)

How is the interest rate determined?

Interest rates are a function of several factors:

- **The market (what others are paying and receiving in interest):** The Federal Reserve (The Fed) sets the baseline on interest rates in the United States by establishing short-term interest rates. Financial institutions and others use that rate as their starting point.

- **The credit risk of the borrower:** Do you, the borrower, have a history of repaying your debts? Bill Gates is probably a pretty safe bet to lend money to, as he can pay back most any amount he borrows. Not so for the unemployed drunk on the street corner. Everybody else will fall somewhere in between those two on the creditworthiness scale.

> The interest rate on U.S. Treasuries is considered to be the risk-free interest rate since the U.S. government is the most creditworthy entity on the planet, at least in 2014. At the rate our debt is increasing, it may not always be that way.

- **The security (if any) on the debt (is the debt attached to an asset?):** A credit card is unsecured, meaning it is not attached to any asset that the lender can take if the borrower doesn't repay the debt. A car loan is secured by the car, but that is riskier collateral than a house because a car can be smashed or driven off into the sunset. A house can burn down, but will have insurance to replace it. A house (used as the borrower's primary residence) is generally considered the best, least risky collateral to secure a loan. Secured loans have a lower interest rate (all other factors being equal) than unsecured loans because there is less risk to the lender.

Here is an example of the interest calculation using different interest payment periods or payment terms:

> The rate and the time period have to match and are quoted as an annual rate so that time is one year.
>
> Amount borrowed: $1,000 on 1/1/14
> Interest rate: 5 percent

> Time period: One year
>
> Terms: Payment at maturity

On 1/1/15 you must pay $50 of interest plus the $1,000 (1,000 x 5 percent x 1 = 50) at the end of that year.

- **Time period:** One month. If instead, you borrow that $1,000 for one month, you have to divide the $50 of interest by 12 months to get the monthly interest. On 2/1/14, you pay 1,004.17 (1,000 x 5 percent x 1/12). You wouldn't say that your rate was 0.4167 percent (5 percent divided by 12) although that math works. It's 5 percent for one month.

- **Terms:** "Interest only" for one year. That means you have to pay the interest part of the loan each month, but you don't pay any of the principal until the end of the term. So you would have to pay $4.17 each month and then at the maturity on 1/1/15 you would repay the $1,000 in a lump sum payment.

- **Amortizing[19]:** If the loan is an amortizing loan, that means you have to pay both principal and interest, in the same total payment amount each month, over the period so that by the end of the year, the loan is totally repaid. You can create an amortization schedule to show the repayments; this one assumes you borrow the money on January 1st:

Pmt No.	Payment Date	Beginning Balance	Scheduled Payment	Extra Payment	Total Payment	Principal	Interest	Ending Balance	Cumulative Interest
1	2/1/14	1000.00	85.61		85.61	81.44	4.17	918.56	4.17
2	3/1/14	918.56	85.61		85.61	81.78	3.83	836.78	7.99

---

19 Amortizing: Type of loan that is set up such that every payment includes both interest payment and principal repayment. A mortgage loan is an amortizing loan. Since the principal is being repaid with each payment, as time goes by, the interest part of the payment will be decreasing while the principal repayment part of the payment will be increasing. The amount of the payment itself stays constant.

Pmt No.	Payment Date	Beginning Balance	Scheduled Payment	Extra Payment	Total Payment	Principal	Interest	Ending Balance	Cumulative Interest
3	4/1/14	836.78	85.61		85.61	82.12	3.49	754.66	11.48
4	5/1/14	754.66	85.61		85.61	82.46	3.14	672.20	14.62
5	6/1/14	672.20	85.61		85.61	82.81	2.80	589.39	17.43
6	7/1/14	589.39	85.61		85.61	83.15	2.46	506.24	19.88
7	8/1/14	506.24	85.61		85.61	83.50	2.11	422.74	21.99
8	9/1/14	422.74	85.61		85.61	83.85	1.76	338.89	23.75
9	10/1/14	338.89	85.61		85.61	84.20	1.41	254.70	25.16
10	11/1/14	254.70	85.61		85.61	84.55	1.06	170.15	26.23
11	12/1/14	170.15	85.61		85.61	84.90	0.71	85.25	26.93
12	1/1/15	85.25	85.61		85.25	84.90	0.36	-	27.29

As you can see, for the first month, P was $1,000 so I was $4.17. However, you had to pay $85.61 in total, so $81.44 was actually a repayment of principal. Now, for the second month, you only had $918.56 in outstanding P at 5 percent for one month so now your interest was down to $3.83 and your principal repayment was $81.78. The last column on the schedule shows the cumulative interest. You can see that you would pay $27.29 in interest over the life of the loan as compared to the $50 when you weren't making any principal repayments.

There are many ways to create an amortization schedule for any debt you carry. You can create one in Excel or go online to find websites with financial calculators. Bankrate.com has many calculators and a lot of useful information. Create amortization schedules for your debt so you can monitor progress on repayment. If you notice in the schedule above, there is a column for "extra payment." Play with adding more to your payment each month and see how it reduces the interest over time and speeds up the repayment. When the numbers are right in front of you, you stay aware of what the debt is costing you. "Out of sight, out of mind" is not a helpful philosophy when it comes to your money.

The Importance of Interest Rate

Compare the example provided with the real-life example of a credit card with a balance of $1,000 at 22.8 percent interest (a good rate on a credit card). In order to pay off that debt, your payment on that $1,000 would be $93.98 and your cumulative interest would be $127.76. That's about $100 dollars more in interest on the same $1,000. The rate is really important, obviously. So that begs the question: how is interest rate determined? The rate is a function of the overall interest environment ("the market"), the credit worthiness of the borrower, the security on the debt (i.e., a car loan is secured by the car whereas a credit card is unsecured), and the purpose of the debt.

The market is what the market is; the debt will either be secured or unsecured, so there isn't much mystery there; the creditworthiness of the borrower is trickier to figure out. In the old days on the prairie, everybody knew whether farmer Joe was rolling in the wheat or a bit down on his luck, and they knew if he was an upstanding guy or a fast-talking shyster. As the world got smaller and people got more mobile, lenders needed a way to quickly tell if somebody had a history of paying or dodging. Say hello to the credit score or FICO.

Your Credit Score

Fair Isaac Corporation (FICO) created the credit scoring system to help lenders know if the borrower is a high or low risk.

The FICO score is made up of several factors:

- **35 percent payment history:** Do you pay on time, all the time?
- **30 percent credit utilization:** Your current outstanding revolving debt divided by total available credit.
- **15 percent length of credit history:** Here's where the old fogies of the world have the advantage. If a Bank X knows that Scott's dad,

Jim, has paid his bills on time for 30 years, the bank feels good that Jim will keep paying in year 31. Scott's two-month history of paying bills on time isn't much to go on.

- **10 percent types of credit used:** There is mortgage debt, consumer finance (car loans), installment (student loans), and revolving (Visa, AmEx). You benefit by being able to effectively manage different types of credit.

- **10 percent recent searches on credit:** Companies search your FICO score in order to give you credit, so if Company F sees that Companies A–E are also looking to give you credit, whoa! You could be ready to go on a spending binge. That's dangerous. You could also be rate shopping (comparing rates between companies A–F). The big, smart computers used by the rating agencies are supposed to figure that out and lump them together as one. It doesn't always work, though.

Each bureau—Equifax, Experian, and TransUnion—can have different data; however, the credit scores they give you should be close to one another. Pull one credit report from one of the bureaus and see where you stand. Use the website annualcreditreport.com.

Examining Your Credit Report

When you get a copy of your credit report, there are a few things you should look out for:

- Is everything accurate?
- Are all of the accounts listed actually yours?
- Are there old accounts listed that you don't use anymore? Close them!
- Are the balances and the details noted from each creditor accurate? For example, if Visa reports that you are "slow pay," is that correct? If not, dispute the details. If anything is not accurate, look on the site for instructions on how to dispute the information and correct errors.

Credit Scores

- Above 750 is excellent.
- Below 620 is considered "risky" by many lenders.

Keep detailed notes about anything you do related to resolving noted issues, such as who you talked to or emailed and when. Put a reminder in your calendar to follow up and see if there has been a response or correction. Also, if you don't have a credit monitoring service, set a calendar reminder to check your credit report annually. You can get one free from each bureau each year, so you could check one of them every four months throughout the year.

Raising Your Credit Score

Your credit report will reveal the factors that negatively influenced your score, so you have a basis for understanding any problems. If you don't have a long credit history, you may want to get a credit card, use it very selectively and, of course, pay off the entire balance on time every month.

In general, raising your credit score is a matter of practicing responsible borrowing and debt management. Here are some tips:

- Pay your bills on time, all the time.
- Get your debt down, especially on credit cards.
- Close accounts that you don't use. Having six gas cards isn't necessary; stick with one or two that you use.
- Fix any errors on your report.
- Write to the bureaus regarding any issues to offer your side of the story. For example, if you lost your job and were unemployed for two months, which might have resulted in some slow pays and late pays during that time period, write a letter to explain the situation, and document the steps you are taking to pay down debt and build up cash reserves to keep you from living paycheck to paycheck in the future.

Perfect isn't expected, but diligence, commitment to honoring your debts, and follow through to recover from problems is.

Credit Cards, Rates, and Minimum Payments

The credit card companies would love for you to carry a big, fat balance on your credit card because they earn interest on that debt every month. Here's a sample credit card statement.

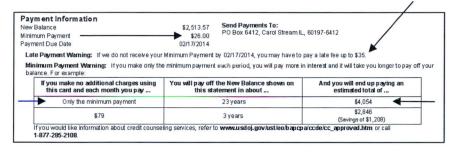

Payment Information

		Send Payments To:
New Balance	$2,513.57	PO Box 6412, Carol Stream IL, 60197-6412
Minimum Payment	$26.00	
Payment Due Date	02/17/2014	

Late Payment Warning: If we do not receive your Minimum Payment by 02/17/2014, you may have to pay a late fee up to $35.

Minimum Payment Warning: If you make only the minimum payment each period, you will pay more in interest and it will take you longer to pay off your balance. For example:

If you make no additional charges using this card and each month you pay ...	You will pay off the New Balance shown on this statement in about ...	And you will end up paying an estimated total of ...
Only the minimum payment	23 years	$4,054
$79	3 years	$2,846 (Savings of $1,208)

If you would like information about credit counseling services, refer to www.usdoj.gov/ust/eo/bapcpa/ccde/cc_approved.htm or call 1-877-285-2108.

The balance owed is **$2,513.57**, and the minimum payment is **$26**. Ridiculous. Nothing will happen if you pay $26 (except that you won't get whacked with a $35 late fee). But at least they are required by law to tell you that if you only make the minimum payment, it will take you 23 years to pay off that balance; 23 years! And, you will pay over $4,000 in interest on that debt. The statement shows an interest rate of 8.24 percent.

Interest Charge Calculation
Your **Annual Percentage Rate (APR)** is the annual interest rate on your account.

Type of Balance	Annual Percentage Rate (APR)	Balance Subject to Interest Rate	Days in Billing Cycle	Interest Charge
PURCHASES	8.24% variable	$0.00	31	$0.00
CASH ADVANCES	19.74%	$0.00	31	$0.00

Note, though, that if you take out cash (cash advance), you will pay 19.74 percent interest. Yikes! It would have to be quite an emergency to borrow money at that rate. In this case, you might as well talk to your friendly neighborhood loan shark.

Paying $54 more than the minimum payment each month drops a measly 20 years off your repayment and saves you $1,200 in interest. That's nice, but think about this: you are still paying $2,846 in interest over those three years. That means that every item you bought as part of that $2,513 cost you more than twice the price you paid. The gas wasn't $3 something a gallon; it was $6 something a gallon. The iPod you bought your sister for Christmas wasn't $300 something; it was $600 something. Anything you thought you were buying on sale really cost you 50 percent more. And that is at 8.24 percent. If your rate was higher, it would take you closer to 30 years to pay the balance (at $47.80/month), and it would cost you $14,695.56 in interest. Holy moly! That loaf of bread was worth its weight in gold.

Debt has a cost, a real-dollars-out-of-your-pocket cost, so understand what you are financing and why, get the best rate you can, and pay more than the minimum payment so you can get rid of the debt as soon as possible.

Financing sweaters and dinners out and the next shiny object will cost you tens of thousands of dollars over your lifetime, probably hundreds of thousands of dollars if you use credit cards consistently. Perhaps you had to finance your college education. Maybe you needed to finance the car you just bought. If you want a house, you will need to finance that too. But understand the consequences—DO THE MATH—create the amortization table (use the Excel template) and see how much you are really paying.

No interest for two years!

Such tempting promotional offers abound from retailers everywhere, especially around the holidays. These offers can be a great way to use someone else's money for months or even years. They can also be a debt trap. The catch is that the interest is accruing in the background. If you miss a payment, pay late, or miss the due date to have the balance paid off, all of the accumulated interest gets charged.

Here is a notice from one bank to transfer credit card balances from other credit cards:

Transfer your higher-rate card balances to your Wells Fargo Credit Card.

If you have credit cards with APRs higher than our special low promotional rate, you may be paying too much. Transfer your balances, manage the number of bills you pay, and reduce the amount of interest you'll pay. It's easy. Here's what you need to do:

- Gather all your credit card bills, including department store and gas cards.

- Check the APR on each one.

- Transfer the balances with APRs higher than our special low promotional rate to your Wells Fargo Credit Card. In addition, a 4% transaction fee ($5 min.) applies to transfers made pursuant to this offer.

- Call **1-800-400-9423** to get the details of your offer.

Take a moment to review your bill and see whether consolidating now is right for you. If you have any questions, we're here to help.

Note the 4 percent transaction fee. On a $1,000 transfer, you pay $40.

Example: You have $1,000 balance at 22.8 percent. You can pay $100/month on that debt. It will take you about a year to pay that off (month 12 payment is $19 so maybe you get it paid in 11 months). Your total interest will be $119.71.

If the promotional transfer rate is 6 percent for one year plus the 4 percent transaction fee, at your $100 payment, you will pay it off in 11 months (month 11 payment is $28.34 so maybe you can pay it off in month 10). Total interest is $28.48, a big difference, but you also pay the $40 fee so you are saving 119.71 − 68.48 = 51.23. Maybe not a life-changing amount, but 50 bucks is 50 bucks!

At ~$200/month payment, you are almost at break-even. Either way it will take you six months to pay it off. Cost of not transferring = 61.09; cost of transferring = 55.28 (15.28 interest + 40 fee). Here you have to decide if the hassle is worth the $6 of savings.

How does that compare to what you pay in interest? What is the savings?

- Understand what the special low promotional rate is and how long it lasts. Typically, these promotional rates give you three to six months at the low rate before the balance returns to the normal rate.
- Project out your payments at that low rate and see if you will pay off the card within that promotional period.
- Call the contact phone number and clarify the details. Ask questions to be sure you completely understand.
- Write down who you spoke to, the date, and the terms discussed. Repeat them back to the rep to be sure you got it right.
- Monitor your progress every month to reassess where you are, pat yourself on the back for milestones achieved, and strategize on how to make it better for next month.

If you take advantage of such an offer:

- Make absolutely, positively sure that you can afford the monthly payment that will pay the balance off within the promotional time period.
- Make absolutely, positively sure that you make every payment on time.
- Watch every payment post to the statement or the online account to be sure it is tracking for payoff.
- Plan to pay off the balance a couple of months early just to know that you won't have a slow mail day cost you that accumulated interest.
- Do not get too many of these going at one time. If you plan to finance a big purchase (furniture, for example), do it piece by piece so that it is manageable, and be sure to factor that in to your monthly cash flow plan.

How Is Your Debt Situation?

Knowledge is power, and an important step toward being smart about debt is knowing where you are. Tell the truth here, accept responsibility for where you are, and forgive yourself if you don't like what you see. It's OK. You are learning and growing, and you have the power to create whatever financial situation you want, but you first have to see where you stand.

In the table below, list every debt (loans, credit cards, mortgage, etc.) that you have:

Who you owe	Balance owed	Minimum monthly payment	Interest rate
Total			

Look at the list you just completed and assess how that makes you feel. Maybe you are really proud because you have almost no debt. Fantastic! Keep doing what you've been doing and work to pay off what little you have.

If looking at this number makes you feel uncomfortable, and you are overwhelmed or feel hopeless about the situation you're in, take a deep breath, and keep reading. There is always a way out. It may not be fun or easy or quick, but it is doable, and the lessons you learn, the experience you gain, will be priceless. Creating a plan and implementing it helps you make progress quickly.

If you are somewhere in between these two extremes, focus on the action plan because you can get to debt-free if that is what you choose.

Basics of a Debt Elimination Plan

- Create a monthly spending plan to make sure you aren't going deeper into debt. Go to Chapter 3 and create your own simple spending plan so you get a handle on where your money is going. Chapter 14 goes in to the nitty gritty of short-term financial goals and cash flow, so that might be helpful for setting realistic goals.

- Remember that five bucks matters. Don't throw things in the shopping cart under the philosophy of "it's only five bucks." Instead, apply that five bucks to your debt payment. Every time you say no to something, tuck that cash in an envelope and pay that much extra on your debt. You'll see the direct benefit of passing up that night out, that concert, or those shoes.

- What role does the rate play in this situation? Some money experts suggest you should pay the most on the highest interest rate debt. Mathematically speaking, sure, but this is a psychology issue, not a math issue. You want to see progress, achievement, something checked off the list as DONE. You will see the fastest progress if you pay off the smallest balance first. This creates achievement, hope, and accomplishment. When you feel good, competent, and in control, you will be inspired to keep going. What you want is consistent positive action and results.

Remember that there will be steps backwards: Cars need repairs, cavities need filling, and people get sick or hurt. Life is what happens while you are making other plans. Regroup, rework the plan, and keep plugging along. Windfalls happen too, so maybe you get a bonus at work or a relative sends you a little bonus cash gift.

Example Plan

Commit your plan to paper or record it on your computer, and put down exactly what you will do, but first look at this example. You will complete this chart by putting in the lowest dollar debt to the highest dollar debt. Assume that once you pay off the first card, you will roll that payment amount toward the next one. Assume today is May 1st:

Who you owe	Balance	Planned* payment	Date it will be paid off	What is my strategy to make this happen?
Macy's	$300	$200 – May	June 15th	Excess cash flow + cut out weekly movie night
		$100 – June		Excess cash flow + cut out weekly movie night
Visa (19.99%)	$550	$20 – May		Pay minimum while I focus on Macy's bill
		$120 – June		Pay the excess not needed on Macy's toward Visa
		$220 – July/Aug	Aug 15th	Roll all of Macy's payment to this debt
Student loan (6.86% over 20 years)	$10,000	$76.69 – May through Aug		Pay minimum payment while I focus on paying off Macy's and Visa
		$300 – September until payoff	12/1/17	Roll the $220 from Macy's and Visa to student loan (plus $3.31 to round it out)

*Does not include interest charges. You can add the interest to each payment (best) or make the extra payment the last month.

Examine the impact of this plan on the student loan. That was set up as a 20-year loan, but by rolling through the extra payments, you reduced it to a four-year-and-seven-month loan. The total interest paid will be $1,441.22 under this plan versus $8,406.03. That's a $7,000 difference! What if you could eke out just $20 more to put toward that student loan payment? You cut off three months, and you would save another $112 in interest. $20 per month is equivalent to about one latte a week. You don't want to live like a monk if you don't have to, but $20 per month?

Before you try working on your own plan, take a look at your last few credit card statements (especially if you carry a balance month-to-month). Look at the charges and think about what you bought. If you want to really geek out, categorize it by "must have" (groceries, gas, etc.) versus "wants," versus "entertainment," and add up the spending for each. Put dining out in the entertainment category. Yes, you must eat, but peanut butter is a must-have; $40 dinners . . . not so much. Now, look at -the interest charge for the month. Was the stuff you bought worth paying that much more?

Time For Your Plan

Fill out the below form for yourself, projecting out what you can do, realistically, to allocate money to your debt. Make sure you have your spending plan handy so you know what is doable and what isn't.

How about identifying some rewards? For each debt that is paid off, do something special for yourself. It doesn't have to be money related, but it can be. You can allocate a portion of the next month's debt pay down to get yourself something special. Enjoy the reward and then buckle down to pay off the next debt. You'll be amazed at how great it feels to have a plan and how much lighter and less stressed you'll feel as the debt balances drop. Keep planning, keep moving forward. You can do it.

Who you owe	Balance	Planned payment	Date it will be paid off	What is my strategy to make this happen?

CHAPTER 6

Income Taxes: April 15th Comes Every Year

In this chapter:

- Federal Return
- Total Worldwide Income
- Adjustments
- Deductions
- Exemptions
- Tax Brackets
- Tax Credits and Liability
- Preparing Your Taxes
- State Return

If you've ever had a job, or ever hope to, you might as well get to know about the Internal Revenue Service (IRS) and what most working Americans view as tax season. The IRS is a federal agency tasked with enforcing the U.S. tax code, and is better known as good old Uncle Sam, the uncle who takes and keeps on taking. He's the opposite of the rich uncle you love to have around.

Remember that federal withholding taken out of your paycheck in Chapter 2? Well, now it's time to see if that withholding was enough to cover your tax liability.

Every working American must file a tax return if they have income in excess of $10,000 for a single taxpayer (2014). The tax return is the final accounting of your income for the year and calculates how much tax you owe (tax liability), then compares it to how much you have paid in (withholdings) to determine if you owe money or get a refund. Tax returns report income earned, deductions, exemptions, and tax credits. The bottom line of the return is how much you owe or get back as a refund. When filing your tax return each year, you need to file a federal tax return and a state tax return unless you live in a state that does not have a state income tax. The returns are due on April 15th each year unless you file for an extension. Filing an extension doesn't alleviate the need to pay the amount you think will be due though, so unless there is a business reason to file an extension, you should just file by April 15th.

Federal Return

The Form 1040 is the main summary form that reports all income, adjustments, total deductions, and the overall tax calculation.

Schedules provide the details behind certain income or deduction items reported on Form 1040 or sometimes on Form 1040A. Form 1040EZ has no supporting schedules or forms.

- Schedule A summarizes all itemized deductions.
- Schedule B summarizes all interest and dividend income.
- Schedule C summarizes all self-employment income and expenses.
- Schedule D summarizes all sales of investments for gain or loss.
- Schedule E summarizes all rental, royalty, partnership (K-1), S Corp, and trust income.
- Schedule F summarizes all income from farming or fishing.
- Schedule SE calculates the amount of self-employment tax you owe and the amount of the adjustment you get.

Basic Tax Formula

	Total worldwide income
−	Adjustments
=	Adjusted gross income
−	Deductions
−	Exemptions
=	Taxable income
x	Income tax rate
=	Income tax
−	Tax credits
=	Tax liability
−	Taxes withheld or paid via estimated payments
=	Amount payable/(refund)

The totals from the schedules will go on Form 1040 on certain line numbers. The form tells you which line number to put the total on, assuming you complete schedules manually. Tax software will automatically add totals to the appropriate numbered line. Form 1040 can also be supported by other forms which generally have a calculation or limitation built in to them.

You can find this formula on Form 1040, which is the most comprehensive form for individual income taxes.

- Form 1040A is a scaled down version of 1040 with limited types of income and adjustments and only the standard deduction, exemptions, and the tax calculation.

- Form 1040EZ is the most basic form with only income, the standard deduction, and exemptions, and, of course, the tax calculation.

Help on Tax Forms

- **Instructions:** Detailed, line-by-line directions on how to complete a specific tax form (i.e., the instructions for Schedule A). For the most part, every form or schedule has instructions
- **Publications:** An IRS overview of a particular topic (i.e., charitable contributions). Charitable contributions are reported on Schedule A, so the Schedule A instructions will tell you on which line to put any charitable contributions and may give a bit of detail about what a charitable contribution is; however, the publication gives you everything you ever wanted to know about what qualifies as a charity, what qualifies as a donation, and what the various limits are for various charities, etc. If your topic is in a publication, there is more to it than meets the eye (lots of rules, limits, and "if/thens").

Total Worldwide Income

This is a pretty easy one. If you received money, except by gift, inheritance, or life insurance proceeds, it is probably taxable income. Twenty bucks of babysitting money? That's taxable income. Five dollar lottery winnings? That's taxable income. Interest income? That's taxable. Earned it in Tijuana? That's still taxable along with your Mozambique income and your middle of Iowa income. Earned illegally? Sorry, that's still taxable, hence the concept of money-laundering, but that's a different subject altogether! The good news is that if you paid taxes in Tijuana or Mozambique, you get a tax credit for those taxes, but we'll save that discussion for later. The bottom line is that it doesn't matter where in the world you earned money, Uncle Sam wants a bite out of it.

The IRS has lots of big, fancy computers to match up what employers paid you with what you report on your tax return. If the numbers don't match, you get a love note from the IRS (officially called an IRS Tax Notification) calculating the amount of tax you owe on the amounts reported through W-2s and or 1099s. Therefore, the IRS computer better find that 1099 income on your tax return somewhere, or it will send you a tax notice telling you to pay more money.

Cash income, which isn't reported on your tax return (getting paid "under the table"), is harder for the IRS to catch; however, the IRS performs a certain percentage of its audits at random. If your number comes up and there are lots of cash deposits to your accounts, they can make you prove that those deposits were not income. If you can't prove it, they can assess it as income, charge you penalties and interest, and maybe even charge you with tax fraud (a criminal offense) for intentionally filing a materially inaccurate return. Honestly, this is why criminals launder money: to avoid the long arm of the IRS. Don't worry too much about a few dollars of lottery winnings but getting substantial cash under the table is fraud plain and simple.

Form W-2: A W-2 is a form which reports your income and withholdings to you and to the IRS. Your employer must provide it to you by January 31st for the prior calendar year.

1099s

- **1099–MISC:** A 1099-MISC means that a company paid you, but you weren't a true employee, you were a contractor. When a company pays you as a contractor, it doesn't withhold any income taxes, and it doesn't pay the employer part of the payroll taxes.

- **1099-B:** Provided by banks and financial institutions to report the sale of investments.

- **1099-DIV:** Provided by banks and financial institutions to report dividend income.

- **1099-G:** Provided by governments to report tax refunds (state) and unemployment benefits.

- **1099-INT:** Provided by banks and financial institutions to report interest income.

- **1099-R:** Provided by banks and financial institutions to report distributions from retirement plans.

- **1099-SSA:** Provided by SSA to report social security payments.

There are others, but these are the most common.

Here's a review of the types of income you could earn. There are two kinds of income: earned income and unearned income. The type of income you earn can matter for some of the tax calculations and limitations.

- Earned income is from your efforts, whether through a job with a W-2, or self-employment income where you get 1099-MISC forms, or whether you self-report. There is a minimum for 1099-MISC reporting of $600/year (2014) so if you earned less than $600 from a company or person, you have to self-report it.

- Unearned income comes from interest, dividends, gain/loss on sales of investments, rental income unless that is your profession (there are lots of rules around real estate professionals), distributions from retirement plans, and other forms of passive activities. Passive essentially means that your money is doing the work for you. There are lots of complicated rules about taking losses from passive activities, but you have to report all your passive income.

On Form 1040, besides W-2 income, 1099 income, and income from Schedules B-F, there are also lines for alimony received, sales of small business property (Form 4797), unemployment compensation, and other (gambling winnings, jury duty fees, and anything that doesn't fit on some other line). Add all of that up and you have Total Income.

> **Did you know?**
> If you don't pay your income taxes, the IRS can garnish[20] your wage and even seize your assets to cover the debt. You will also pay penalties and interest. You can even go to prison for tax evasion if you "willfully and fraudulently" underreport your income. Just ask Al Capone.

---

20 Garnish: Legal process of making an employer take money from the employee's paycheck to repay debts. The IRS can garnish wages to recover tax liabilities. Courts can garnish for unpaid child support or other legal obligations that are unpaid.

Adjustments

Adjustments are expenses that you paid during the tax year that Congress legislated to be a reduction of your total worldwide income on a dollar-for-dollar basis for income tax purposes. The adjustments as of the 2014 tax year are:

- **Educator expenses**: This allows teachers to reduce their income for amounts spent on classroom supplies that they pay for. Limited to $250.

- Certain business expenses of reservists, performing artists, and fee-basis government officials: See Form 1040 instructions if you fit these narrow categories (Form 2106).

- **Health Savings Account (HSA):** This is where you reduce income for your contributions to your HSA. See Chapter 2 for details (Form 8889).

- **Moving expenses:** When you move more than 50 miles for a new job, you may get an adjustment for those expenses. You have to complete Form 3903 to determine the amount of the adjustment.

- **Deductible part of self-employed taxes:** When you are self-employed, you (as your own employer) have to pay the employer part of Social Security taxes for yourself (as well as the employee part). This is called a self-employment tax. You calculate your self-employment tax on Schedule SE. Then you get an adjustment for half of the amount you paid.

Did you know?

When Congress wants to encourage certain types of spending, it creates a positive income tax effect for taxpayers. This comes in the form of adjustments to income, tax deductions, or tax credits. Beware! Many of these have phase-outs based on adjusted gross income, which means that once you go over a certain amount of income, your adjustment is reduced or eliminated completely.

- **Self-employed SEP, simple, and qualified plan contributions:** This is an adjustment for retirement plan contributions when you are self-employed. There is no phase-out, but there are limits to how much you can contribute in a year, based on plan type. It is always limited to earned income.

- **Self-employed health insurance premiums:** As it sounds, you can adjust your income for the amount of your health insurance premiums when you are self-employed.

- **Penalty on early withdrawal of savings (CDs):** Certificates of deposit are a form of safe investment that pays a higher rate of interest than a savings account but requires you to hold the CD for a certain period of time as quoted in the contract. If you withdraw your money before the term is reached, you pay a penalty. You do get an adjustment for the amount of the penalty.

- **Alimony paid:** If you are divorced and paying alimony (not child support) to your ex-spouse, you get an adjustment and the ex-spouse must include it as income.

- **IRA contributions:** If you make a contribution to an individual retirement account, you get an income adjustment. It is limited to $5,500 (2014) and there is a phase-out based on income. See Chapter 10 or IRS publication 590 for details.

- **Student loan interest deduction:** As it sounds, this is interest paid on student loans. This does phase out based on income, so check the instructions on Form 1040 if you are manually preparing your return.

- **Tuition and fees:** You may get an adjustment for certain tuition and fees paid for you or a dependent. There is a phase out based on income so check out Form 8879 to see if you qualify.

- **Domestic production activities deduction:** This is a very specific adjustment for U.S. manufacturing and software companies that paid wages in the United States. Check out Form 8903 if you have a small manufacturing or software business.

Now that you've found your total income and subtracted your total adjustments, you've arrived at a number that represents your adjusted gross income (AGI). AGI is important because a lot of limitations and calculations are based on AGI. For tax purposes, a low AGI is good. For living-your-life-comfortably purposes, the higher the better.

Deductions

Deductions are categories of expense that you get to subtract from your AGI before you calculate the amount of tax you owe.

Itemized Deductions

- Medical expenses (limited)
- Certain taxes paid
- Mortgage interest
- Gifts to charity
- Casualty and theft losses
- Job expenses and miscellaneous items (limited)

There are two options for taking deductions:

1. **Standard deduction:** An amount established in the tax code as a "standard" amount that you can deduct from AGI. It is based on your filing status (addressed later in this chapter). If you are not married and don't have children, your filing status will be single. As a single person, you can automatically deduct $6,100 (2014) even if you have no itemized deductions.

2. **Itemized deductions:** Itemized deductions are specific items that the tax code says are deductible from your AGI. This is Congress' way of "incenting" Americans to spend money in a certain way.

   - **Medical expenses:** When you incur medical and dental expenses, you are allowed to deduct the amounts of your out-of-pocket expenses. However, you only get to deduct the amount that is greater than 7.5 percent (2014) of your AGI. Unless you have very high medical expenses or very low AGI, you probably won't get a deduction here.

   - **Taxes paid:** If you paid state or local income taxes, real estate taxes, or certain other property taxes (usually on vehicles), you get to deduct the amount you actually paid, or had withheld, during the tax year. If your state doesn't have an income tax, you can take a deduction for sales tax if you live in a state with sales tax. There are tables available to help you determine how much sales tax deduction you can take based on your income (there's no need to save every store receipt!).

- **Mortgage interest:** If you own your own home and paid interest on a mortgage, you can deduct the amount you paid. Your mortgage company will send you a Form 1098 in January showing the amount you paid.

- **Gifts to charity:**

  - **Cash contributions to qualified charities:** You can usually deduct the amount you donated within certain limitations. Generally, for a cash donation to a recognized public charity, you can deduct the whole contribution up to your AGI. There is a carry-forward if you can't take the whole deduction in the current year. A carry-forward is a provision in the tax code which lets you use the deduction in a future tax year if you are unable to use the whole amount in the current tax year.

  - **Non-cash contributions (usually household items or clothing) to public charities:** You can take the thrift store value of the items. Any contribution in excess of $500 will require another form and a lot more documentation. See Form 8283 and its instructions for more details.

    - □ If you gift investments, you can deduct the average market value of the investment on the date of gift. For example, you gave 100 shares of ABC company stock. The quoted market price on the date of the gift showed a high of $10 and a low of $9.50. You can deduct 100 X $9.75 or $975.

      □ Gifts to nonpublic charities, such as a private foundation, have further restrictions. See IRS Publication 526 for more details on charitable gifts and their deductibility.

- **Casualty and theft losses**: If you have a big-ticket item stolen or you suffer a loss due to a fire, flood, or other disaster, you may get a tax adjustment for the amount of your loss that exceeds certain limits. You do have renter's or homeowner's insurance to cover most of that, right? See Chapter 7 for more on insurance. Even with insurance, you may have a casualty adjustment, so check IRS Publication 547 for details on how this is calculated and what types of losses qualify.

- **Job expenses and miscellaneous deductions:** These are expenses related to your job for which you were not reimbursed. Miscellaneous expenses include the cost of preparing your tax return as well as a few very narrowly defined specialty items. You only get to deduct job and miscellaneous expenses that are greater than 2 percent of AGI (2014). See Publication 529 for all the details.

Exemptions

Exemptions are amounts determined by the tax code based on how many people your income is supporting. Each taxpayer has his or her own exemption, so if you are married and file a joint return, both you and your spouse get an exemption. In 2014, exemptions are worth $3,950. This is a direct reduction of AGI. You also get an exemption for each dependent you claim on your tax return.

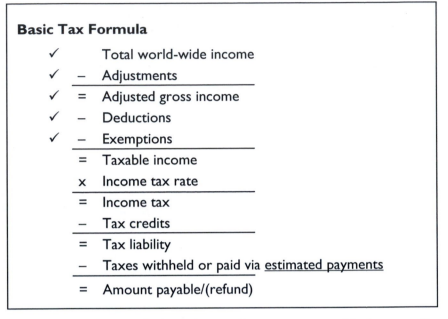

Basic Tax Formula
- ✓   Total world-wide income
- ✓ − Adjustments
- ✓ = Adjusted gross income
- ✓ − Deductions
- ✓ − Exemptions
  - = Taxable income
  - × Income tax rate
  - = Income tax
  - − Tax credits
  - = Tax liability
  - − Taxes withheld or paid via estimated payments
  - = Amount payable/(refund)

The next task is to calculate the tax due on your taxable income. To calculate the total tax liability, you first need to understand filing status.

Filing status is the category used by the IRS tax code to determine how much tax you will owe on your taxable income considering your marital status and family situation.

Single, married filing jointly (MFJ), and married filing separately (MFS) are pretty straightforward. You should be aware that if you are married and you elect to file separately, you will likely pay more tax than if you filed jointly. The phase-outs for certain adjustments, deductions, or credits are much lower for MFS and certain tax benefits are lost completely for MFS. Of course, there may be valid reasons you don't want to file with your spouse, but be sure to calculate the tax both ways to determine the impact.

Filing status categories:

- Single individual
- Married person filing jointly or surviving spouse
- Married person filing separately

- Head of household (HOH) is available for a person who is not married but who supports dependents. Dependent status is straightforward if the person is your child under the age of 19 (24 for a full-time student) and you provide more than half of his or her support during the year. It can get more complicated in divorce situations or when the support is for someone other than your own child. See the instructions to Form 1040 for a complete analysis and decision tree regarding determination of dependency.

- Qualifying widow(er) with dependent children (QW) is reserved for a person whose spouse has died within the last two years and who supports dependent children. Note on timing: In the year of the spouse's death, you would likely file as married filing jointly if that was your previous filing status. In the following two years, you would file as QW with dependent children, assuming that you have dependent children. If you do not have dependent children, you would file as single in the year following your spouse's death.

Tax Brackets

This is the range of taxable income that is calculated by applying a set tax rate.

2014 Tax Rates & Tax Brackets

The IRS released the final 2014 tax brackets. Here are the federal 2014 tax tables:

Tax Rate	Single	Married Filing Joint	Married Filing Separate	Head of Household
10%	Up to $9,075	Up to $18,150	Up to $9,075	Up to $12,950
15%	$9,076 – $36,900	$18,151 – $73,800	$9,076 – $36,900	$12,951 – $49,400
25%	$36,901 – $89,350	$73,801 – $148,850	$36,901 – $74,425	$49,401 – $127,550
28%	$89,351 – $186,350	$148,851 – $226,850	$74,426 – $113,425	$127,551 – $206,600
33%	$186,351 – $405,100	$226,851 – $405,100	$113,426 – $202,550	$206,601 – $405,100
35%	$405,101 – $406,750	$405,101 – $457,600	$202,551 – $228,800	$405,101 – $432,200
39.6%	Over $406,750	Over $457,600	Over $228,800	Over $432,200

The 2014 federal tax tables are based on your filing status and number of dependents for the 2014 calendar year.

The important thing to understand about the tax brackets is that regardless of how much your taxable income is, the first $9,075 (2014) is only taxed at 10 percent. The next $27,824 is taxed at 15 percent and so on. We refer to your bracket as the marginal tax rate to indicate the rate applied to your last dollar of taxable income. So if you had taxable income of $42,503, your marginal rate would be 25 percent.

The effective rate is your total tax liability divided by your total income. This takes into consideration your adjustments, deductions, exemptions, tax credits, and the graduated tax rates.

There are a couple of wrinkles in the tax rate calculation:

Qualified Dividends and Capital Gains Rate
If some of your income came from qualified dividends (your 1099 will tell you if it is qualified or not) or capital gains (you sold a capital asset like stocks or bonds at a gain), the tax code taxes you at a reduced rate as compared to ordinary income. Use the Qualified Dividends and Capital Gains Tax Worksheet found conveniently in the 214-page instructions to form 1040.

Alternative Minimum Tax
The Tax Code adds back "Preference Items" like the state taxes that you deducted on Schedule A as well as some other things and does a whole separate calculation of tax under this alternative method. If you owe more tax under that method, you have to pay using that approach. Alt Min is calculated on Form 6251. Don't worry, the instructions for this form are only 13 pages long.

Or you can just use tax software and let it do all this math for you.

Here is where you stand on the tax formula:

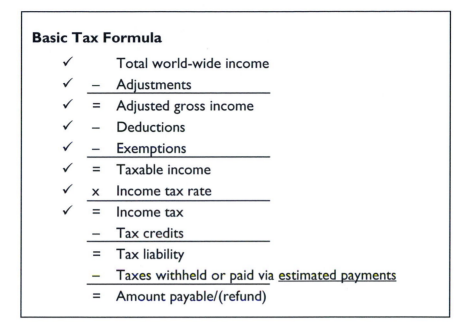

Basic Tax Formula
- ✓   Total world-wide income
- ✓   –   Adjustments
- ✓   =   Adjusted gross income
- ✓   –   Deductions
- ✓   –   Exemptions
- ✓   =   Taxable income
- ✓   x   Income tax rate
- ✓   =   Income tax
-      –   Tax credits
-      =   Tax liability
-      –   Taxes withheld or paid via estimated payments
-      =   Amount payable/(refund)

Tax Credits and Liabilities

Tax credits reduce your tax on a dollar-for-dollar basis. While adjustments, deductions, and exemptions all decrease taxable income—which certainly helps to reduce taxes—tax credits actually reduce the tax itself so they are much more valuable and, you guessed it, harder to qualify for. Here is a list of the tax credits available as of the 2014 tax year and a basic description of how to qualify for them. Note that some have a phase out.

- **Foreign tax credit (Form 1116):** If you had to pay taxes in a foreign country, you get a credit for those taxes. Before you automatically think that this doesn't apply, consider your investments. If you have a mutual fund that invests in international equities, the mutual fund may have had to pay foreign taxes on some of the income. As an owner, that means you had to pay some foreign taxes. Luckily, your 1099 will clearly show the foreign tax paid. Form 1116 is used in certain situations, but you can also elect not to use it.

- **Credit for child and dependent care expenses (Form 2441):** This credit may apply if you have a child or another dependent (parent, disabled spouse, etc.) who requires care while you work. There is, of course, a limit to the amount of the credit. See Publication 503 for details on the credit. In 2014, the credit is a percentage of eligible expenses. The maximum eligible expense is $3,000 per dependent for up to two dependents.

- **Education Credits (Form 8863):** Not eligible for the credit at AGI above $90,000 (S) or $180,000 (MFJ) or if filing MFS. This is an example of a "penalty" if you are married and using filing status "separate" as opposed to "joint." You lose the ability to apply this credit. Here is a really great summary of education credits found in the instructions to Form 8863:

Table 1. **Comparison of Education Credits**

Caution. You can claim both the American opportunity credit and the lifetime learning credit on the same return-but not for the same student.

	American Opportunity Credit	Lifetime Learning Credit
Maximum credit	Up to $2,500 credit per eligible student	Up to $2,000 credit per return
Limit on modified adjusted gross income (MAGI)	$180,000 if married filing jointly; $90,000 if single, head of household, or qualifying widow(er)	$124,000 if married filing jointly; $62,000 if single, head of household, or qualifying widow(er)
Refundable or nonrefundable	40% of credit may be refundable; the rest is nonrefundable	Nonrefundable—credit limited to the amount of tax you must pay on your taxable income
Number of years of postsecondary education	Available **ONLY** if the student had not completed the first 4 years of postsecondary education before 2012	Available for all years of postsecondary education and for courses to acquire or improve job skills
Number of tax years credit available	Available **ONLY** for 4 tax years per eligible student (including any year(s) Hope credit was claimed)	Available for an unlimited number of years
Type of program required	Student must be pursuing a program leading to a degree or other recognized education credential	Student does not need to be pursuing a program leading to a degree or other recognized education credential
Number of courses	Student must be enrolled at least half time for at least one academic period beginning during the year	Available for one or more courses
Felony drug conviction	As of the end of 2012, the student had not been convicted of a felony for possessing or distributing a controlled substance	Felony drug convictions do not make the student ineligible
Qualified expenses	Tuition, required enrollment fees, and course materials that the student needs for a course of study whether or not the materials are bought at the educational institution as a condition of enrollment or attendance	Tuition and required enrollment fees (including amounts required to be paid to the institution for course-related books, supplies, and equipment)
Payments for academic periods	Payments made in 2012 for academic periods beginning in 2012 or beginning in the first 3 months of 2013	

Jan 11, 2013   Cat. No. 53002G

- **Retirement savings contributions credit (Form 8880):** This credit applies to people who made contributions to qualified retirement plans such as IRAs, Roth IRAs, or 401(k) plans. You do not qualify for the credit if adjusted gross income is above $30,000 (S), $45,000 (HOH), or $60,000 (MFJ) (2014).

- **Child tax credit (Form 8812):** This is a credit for having a child under the age of 17. It doesn't even begin to cover the cost of having the little cherub, but it is worth taking. The maximum credit is $1,000 and it phases out at higher income levels.

- **Residential energy credits (Form 5695):** This credit applies to improvements to your home to make it more energy efficient. Take a look at this if you made improvements. Frequently, the vendor who sold the product will loudly and proudly announce that the product qualifies for this credit.

- **General business credit (Form 3800):** If you have a small business and qualify for these very specific and targeted credits, you would use this form to report them. These credits include "Nonconventional source fuel credit" and "Qualified railroad track maintenance credit." See the instructions to form 3800 for a complete list. If you have a unique business, are in an economically disadvantaged area, or utilize alternative fuel sources, there may be a credit available to you.

- **Earned Income Credit (Schedule EIC):** A refundable credit available for people who work and earn lower incomes. It is essentially an incentive for people to work, as they can offset income tax owed or actually receive money back. To qualify, 2014 AGI cannot exceed $14,590 (single, no children) up to $52,427 (married, three children). The credit is calculated on Worksheet A of Form 1040 (see instructions).

> **Refundable credit:** You get the credit even if you don't owe or pay any income tax. Think, think . . . the government is actually paying you. Examples are earned income credit (EIC) and up to 40 percent of the American Opportunity Tax Credit (tuition). If you are in either of these situations, it's pretty likely that you aren't earning very much money.

And those are your federal tax credits for individuals. Give them a big hand; they work hard to save you money!

If you think any of those might be applicable to you, go to the IRS website and search for the instructions to the form (under forms and publications, type only the form number in the search box, and you should get the form and the instructions). If there aren't any instructions, they are probably part of the instructions to Form 1040, so check there.

With the tax credits safely behind you, now take another look at the formula.

The tax liability is simply the calculated income tax less those lovely tax credits.

Basic Tax Formula

✓		Total world-wide income
✓	−	Adjustments
✓	=	Adjusted gross income
✓	−	Deductions
✓	−	Exemptions
✓	=	Taxable income
✓	×	Income tax rate
✓	=	Income tax
✓	−	Tax credits
	=	Tax liability
	−	Taxes withheld or paid via estimated payments
	=	Amount payable/(refund)

Now, subtract what your employer withheld from your pay (shown on your W-2) or that you paid in for yourself in the form of estimated payments. The result is what you owe in additional taxes or what the government owes you back in the form of a refund. The goal is to be close to $0. That means you aren't crying about having to write a check, and you haven't given Uncle Sam an interest-free loan in the form of withdrawals from your paycheck throughout the year.

What if you owe more?

- Consider contributing money to a traditional IRA. There are restrictions; see Chapter 10. This is an adjustment to income and will lower your taxes.

- Write the check. It has to be done.

- If you can't pay it, set up an installment plan.

- Increase your withholding. See your payroll rep about filling out a new W-4. Your other choice is to make estimated payments every 4/15, 6/15, 9/15, and 1/15 to avoid having a liability next year.

What if you get a refund?

Yippee!

- Consider contributing the refund to a Roth IRA (at least some of it). There are restrictions. See Chapter 10.

- Decrease your withholding to try to get closer to $0. Then set up an automatic transfer, every pay period, into your savings account, or better yet, your Roth IRA. Same net pay, but now you are boosting your savings. No need to let Uncle Sam use your money all year.

This whole tax thing is painful, painful, painful. The paying is bad enough, but doing the return, the hassle of it all, yuck. But it is really important that you file your tax return if you make over $10,000 (2014) as a single person (MFJ is $20,000). The instructions to the tax forms will tell you who must file, so check there if you aren't sure.

The IRS gets really cranky when you don't file your return or don't pay the amount due (or apply for a payment plan). The IRS can garnish your wages, confiscate money from your bank account, or seize other assets. It's best to file your return, pay your taxes, and live a happy life without fearing a letter from Uncle Sam.

Did you know?

According to the IRS website, "The failure-to-file penalty is generally more than the failure-to-pay penalty." They definitely want you to show up.

As if the federal return wasn't "taxing" enough, now you have to prepare the state return.

State Return

State income tax calculations can vary widely:

- No individual income taxes: Alaska, Florida, Nevada, New Hampshire, South Dakota, Tennessee (tax on income from stocks and bonds only), Texas, Washington, Wyoming.
- Flat tax (no "tiers" like the federal system provides).
- Graduated tax rates ("tiers" based on taxable income).
- Tax calculation that starts with a federal "base" such as taxable income or AGI.
- Tax calculation that is nothing like the federal system.

If you live in a state that does assess income taxes, go to the state's department of revenue website and search for information about individual income taxes. There is probably a "general information" section that provides basic information. Here is what the Georgia DOR says:

Good job Georgia! This tells you quite a bit:

- the system is graduated (meaning that tax is assessed at different rates depending on taxable income),
- the system is based on federal AGI,
- everybody pays, and
- retirees get a break by being able to exclude some income.

Individual Income Tax

There is a link to access actual tax forms and the instruction book to get a general idea about all the particulars of your state tax return. The form lays out the overall flow pretty well:

> Federal AGI
> +/– Adjustments from Schedule 1
> = Georgia AGI
> – Deductions (either the Georgia standard deduction or federal itemized deductions less adjustments)
> – Exemptions (defined by Georgia)
> = Georgia taxable income

Calculate the tax based on the rate schedules

	Credits from Schedule 2
=	Total state tax
−	Amount withheld or paid via estimated payments
=	Amount due or amount to be refunded

That's pretty easy since it is much like the federal system. You would then dig in to Schedule 1 to see what adjustments you have to make to income, understand the adjustments to itemized deductions and, of course, carefully examine Schedule 2 since it relates to tax credits.

Do a review for your state and see what information you can find to give you the big picture view.

Preparing Your Taxes

Obviously, discussing your tax situation with a professional is always helpful, but even if you do that, educate yourself first so you can ask some relevant questions. Make sure you have a basic understanding of taxes. Always review your own return to make sure you get it. You are the one on the hook for any errors or omissions on the return.

Tax Prep Options

- **Fill out the forms yourself (paper or online):** This is a good option if you just have a W-2, have no dependents, and are taking the standard deduction. It's easy, free, and you get a better understanding of the process of completing the forms.

- **Use purchased tax software:** This is a good option if you have more complexity such as a house, kids, etc., but your situation is not so complex that you need professional help. It's a pain to sit down and do it and there is some expense involved, but it's good to see how everything comes together.

- **Pay a preparer:** A CPA will be much more expensive than purchasing software, but you have a pro on your team. Hiring a tax preparer is a must if you have your own business, have anything foreign, or do a lot of complex charitable contributions. If you go to a "tax in a box" place, ask a lot of questions of your preparer. Some are really great and some were trained last week.

The Details of Your Return

Supporting the information on your tax return is as important as preparing it. Get a file folder or envelope labeled 20YY taxes. Put every piece of paper that relates to your income or your adjustments and deductions into the folder. If you are an over-achiever, have different folders for income, adjustments, and deductions. This simple process will make preparing your tax return much easier because you will have all of your support documents in one place. Of course, you can use an electronic system for keeping receipts, but make sure it is backed up.

The bottom line on tax return support is that if you get audited, can you prove to the IRS agent that you actually paid those expenses you deducted and that they were valid? He who documents best, wins. So keep copies of your return after you file it and keep all of the supporting receipts with it, stored in a safe place. Hopefully the IRS won't come calling, but if they do, you'll be prepared.

That does it for income taxes. Isn't being an adult fun? And speaking of fun, it's time to jump into insurance, where you get to pay for something intangible and hope you never use what you just paid for. Awesome!

CHAPTER 7

Insurance

In this chapter:

- Insurance Companies
- The Language of Insurance
- Types of Insurance and Who Needs Them
- Getting a Quote

Insurance is something that you hate to have to write a check for, but you will love if you ever need to file a claim. The theory behind insurance is that if many people pay the insurance company small amounts each month (the premium), then the insurance company can pay the few people who actually incur an expensive loss. Think of your car. If you get in an accident, you couldn't afford to pay $5,000, $10,000, or more to cover the cost to repair the car. But you (and millions of other people) can afford to pay a few hundred a month for the insurance. You hope you won't smash your car, but if you do, someone else will pay to get it fixed.

Purpose of Insurance: to pass your risk of financial loss on to someone else.

- Someone else (the insurance company) wants money (the premium) for assuming this risk.

- You pay the small amount (the premium) to ensure that you get a big amount (the value lost) if something big, bad, and ugly happens.

- You only want to insure the big losses that you can't afford to cover personally.

- The downside to the insurance is that you might pay the premiums for years and never once have an insured loss. In fact, that is what you hope happens.

What you are actually paying for is peace of mind.

Insurance Companies

As with all things in life, it matters who you do business with. Shady Sam on the street corner is not likely to provide good service after the sale; ditto with Joe's Fly-by-Night Insurance Company. As Allstate so aptly states in its "mayhem" commercials, "Your cut-rate insurance company may not pay for this." You can (and should) check out the insurance company's rating before you give them your money.

Name recognition is not necessarily relevant when choosing an insurance company. There are good companies that don't spend a lot of money on national advertising. Insurance companies are regulated by the states, so you can go to your state insurance regulator's website and get information as well.

- A.M. Best rates insurance companies in terms of credit worthiness (do they have the financial assets to pay their claims?).

- J.D. Power does consumer surveys that provide insight into how customer friendly insurance companies are. You don't want a company that makes you jump through a bunch of hoops to get anything paid.

- thestreet.com gives financial health ratings of many companies (banks, insurance companies, etc.), and is therefore a reputable authority. A "D"-rated company is probably not one you can count on to be there in 20 years when you need a disability or life policy paid out.

The Language of Insurance

- **Actual cash value** is what the insurance company would pay for the value of the covered item on the day it was damaged or destroyed. Contrast that with replacement cost coverage (RCC) which will pay to replace the item. Example: You own a 15-year-old beat up car that gets totaled in an accident. The actual value of the car is $700. If it is insured for actual value, you get $700. Rats! There's no way you can replace your car for $700. Unfortunately, you can't get car insurance that replaces a car, even though some ads claim they cover new car replacement, presumably for some limited period of time.

- **Cash surrender value (CSV)** is an account that can build up with a permanent life insurance policy which is created because you pay premiums in excess of the cost of the insurance.

- **Insurability** is the ability to be insured (duh). However, life, health, disability, or long-term care insurance have criteria that you must meet in order to be insurable. Someone with a terminal illness is not insurable. Someone with a chronic illness may be insurable by one company but not another depending on the criteria set by the company.

- **Premium** is the amount paid annually, quarterly, or monthly to insure the covered risk.

- **Indemnity** is protection against loss. To indemnify is to "make whole again" so the purpose of the insurance is that you are put back to where you were before the loss, no better, no worse.

- **Perils** are the cause of losses. Insurance will cover specific perils.

- **Hazards** are things or situations which increase the risk of loss from a peril.

- **Covered losses** are the types of loss that the insurer will indemnify you for. Not all losses to a covered item are insured. Example: Most homeowner's insurance does not cover loss from floods. You must specifically buy flood insurance to cover that risk.

- **Exclusions** are types of losses that are not covered under the insurance policy. Loss from a war is not covered, for example.

- **Claim** is the method of notifying the insurance company that a covered loss has been incurred. Try not to file claims on your policy. Filing numerous claims impacts the cost your insurance in the future.

- **Coverage limits** are the maximum amount the insurer will pay out under the policy. There are limits by occurrence and for the policy.

- **Deductible** is the amount you pay toward the loss before the insurer starts to pay. The higher the deductible, the lower the premium. This is essentially determining how much risk of loss you are willing to bear. Set your deductible as high as you can afford to since you are only insuring losses beyond what you can financially bear.

- **Replacement cost coverage (RCC)** is the payment by the insurer to replace the covered item regardless of its value at the time it was damaged or destroyed. Contrast that with "actual cash value" (ACV) which only pays you for the item's value. Example: On homeowner's insurance, you insure at replacement value because you need to have the home rebuilt if it burns down. RCC will be more expensive than ACV.

- **Rider** is an add-on coverage for extra benefits or to insure items of higher than average value like firearms, collections, jewelry, furs, etc.

- **Underwriting** is the insurance company's process of evaluating you, your situation, and your risk of loss. They use this information to decide if they should accept or decline to insure you and also to determine how much your premium will be based on the likelihood that they will have to pay out claims under the policy. Someone with three car accidents in three years will have a hard time getting insurance. Do you want to insure her in year four? No thanks. You might not even want to ride with her!

- **Policy.** Before you determine the type of insurance you need, you should understand the primary document used for insurance. An insurance policy is the legal document (contract) that describes the terms of the insurance, including what is being insured, what perils are covered, and the term of the insurance. The policy has the following sections:

  - **Declarations page:** The first page of the policy that provides a summary of the terms—who, what, how long, how much, what price.

  - **Insuring agreement:** The heart of the policy which lays out the terms, specifically what the insurer will do to indemnify you for covered losses.

  - **Exclusions:** Those losses which are not covered by the policy. This is critical to know.

  - **Conditions:** The rules and procedures for you and the insurer, such as how to make a claim, how to cancel the policy, what to do after a loss, and how disagreements are handled.

  - **Endorsements:** An amendment to a policy to cover something specific that would not normally be covered under the policy. This could be extra coverage or adding a person to your policy. This will change the premium. It is still considered part of the policy, but extends the basic policy.

Terms Specific To Disability

- **Benefit period.** How long will the benefit pay you? The longest term is until full retirement age as defined by social security. This is the most expensive. One way to reduce the premium cost is to pick a shorter benefit period. It is not ideal, but even a five-year benefit is better than none and would give you time to figure out a new plan, get trained for a different type of job, sell an expensive house, etc. in the event that you were disabled. Long-term care policies will also have a benefit period.

- **Elimination period.** This is the period of time between becoming disabled and starting the payment of benefits—essentially the risk that you assume prior to the insurance company taking on the risk. A longer elimination period will reduce the premium, but you have to be able to cover your own expenses during that period. The most common elimination period is 90 days. Long-term care policies will have an elimination period as well.

- **Renewability.** It is important to understand the variety of options.

  - Noncancelable means you have the right to renew the policy at the same rate until age 65. This is a great feature, but will add to the cost of the premium.

  - Guaranteed renewable means the insurance company can increase the premium for every policyholder in that entire insurance category, but not on an individual basis (they can't increase only your insurance premium). There is more risk here, but the initial premium is lower than in a noncancelable.

  - Conditionally renewable is when there are conditions for renewal that may raise the rates on this type of plan. This is the most risky, yet carries a smaller initial premium.

Types of Insurance and Who Needs Them

- **Life:** Anyone who has people depending on them or their income in order to survive (parents with children, a person supporting a disabled spouse, a parent with a disabled child, someone supporting elderly parents, etc.) or someone who wishes to leave money to a person or charity upon their death.

- **Health:** Everyone who is not financially independent and does not have the resources to cover millions of dollars of catastrophic medical care.

- **Disability:** Anyone who works and is dependent upon that income for their support.
- Property and casualty (P&C):
  - **Personal property:** Any other kind of property that would be found inside of real property like furniture, computers, clothing, etc. (excludes any kind of motor craft like cars, boats, etc.). If you have stuff (clothing, computers) that you can't afford to replace, you want this coverage. The policy would likely be renter's insurance if you do not own a home. The personal property inside a home that you own is covered by your homeowner's policy.
  - **Real property (buildings, structures like fences, and land):** Anyone who owns a home will want homeowner's insurance, and mortgage companies require it because the home is their collateral for the loan.
- **Commercial property:** Anyone who owns business property and cannot afford to replace it needs this coverage. It pays upon damage or destruction of business property.
- **Automobile:** Anyone who owns a car needs an auto policy. This coverage pays upon damage or destruction of a car; can be either personal or business, and the classification will matter with respect to the terms, coverages, and premiums.
- **Liability:** Anyone who functions in society needs some basic liability coverage (hermits need not apply). Liability is part of homeowner's, renter's, and auto policies, but you can also purchase an umbrella policy that covers liability in excess of the limits of those policies.
- **Long-term care:** Anyone who does not have the financial resources to pay for nursing home care or in-home assistance in their old age. Usually, it is recommended to consider this type of coverage in your 50s.

These are the basic types of insurance that you will likely need during your lifetime. If you own a business, there are other types of insurance to consider related to your business activities. If you are in that situation, you will want to discuss these types of insurance with an agent who specializes in business insurance.

Life

There are a number of life insurance products in the marketplace, and more variations may continue to evolve. Group term insurance was mentioned in Chapter 2 in the section on employee benefits. If your employer offers any type of group life insurance, that is the best place to start, as the rates are usually pretty reasonable. The downside of this type of coverage is that it usually terminates when you quit. If you move to another company that offers this benefit, you should be able to sign up there.

Types of life insurance

Term	Death benefit	Fixed at amount you request
	Term length	10, 15, 20 or 30 years
	Premium	Fixed, level for term
	CSV accumulation	No
	Investment of CSV	N/A
	Cancellation	Any time without penalty
	Comments	Inexpensive for the young and healthy
Whole Life	Death benefit	Fixed at amount you request
	Term length	Life (age 100)
	Premium	Fixed level, but much more expensive than term for the same benefit
	CSV accumulation	Yes—accumulates a cash value that can be borrowed
	Investment of CSV	Interest on the balance at rate set by insurance company; tax-deferred
	Cancellation	Any time, but you may forfeit the CSV if you cancel too soon into the policy life
	Comments	Expensive since part of the premium is really "savings" of cash

Universal	Death benefit	Can be adjusted over time
	Term length	Life (age 100)
	Premium	Can vary; increases will increase CSV and death benefit; decreases will reduce them.
	CSV accumulation	Yes—accumulates a cash value that can be borrowed or used to "pay the premium" if it is sufficient
	Investment of CSV	Interest on the balance at rate set by insurance company; tax-deferred
	Cancellation	Any time but you may forfeit the CSV if you cancel too soon into the policy life
	Comments	Expensive since part of the premium is really "savings" of cash
Variable Universal	Death benefit	Can be adjusted over time
	Term length	Life (age 100)
	Premium	Can vary; increases will increase CSV and death benefit; decreases will reduce them.
	CSV accumulation	Yes—accumulates a cash value that can be borrowed or used to "pay the premium" if it is sufficient
	Investment of CSV	Allows you to invest in mutual funds and get market appreciation on your CSV
	Cancellation	Any time but you may forfeit the CSV if you cancel too soon into the policy life
	Comments	Expensive as any permanent policy and dangerous. If the market crashes, you may need to pay in money to keep the death benefit.

So which do you pick?

As with all financial decisions, it depends. There are situations for which a permanent life insurance policy makes some sense, but for someone young and just starting out, you might want to keep it simple. Buy the most term insurance you can afford for the longest term you can get, and then start saving and investing. The goal for most people is to get rich. When you are rich (financially independent), you probably don't need life insurance because you have sufficient assets to provide for the people who are depending on you. At that point, you cancel the term insurance, and you aren't spending money to insure that risk.

The benefit of permanent insurance is that it can last your whole life if you keep paying the premium, so you never have to worry that a term expires and you can't get another policy for some reason. They are expensive, though, and the buildup of a cash value is a false promise. You can build up your own cash balance for free. Why pay an insurance company to hold your money for you and bear the risk of needing to get it before the surrender period ends? Yes, the investment income is tax-deferred, but until you are fully funding your 401(k) and IRA, you have the ability to create the tax-deferred investment gains on those accounts.

Life insurance people will tell you that the benefit of permanent insurance is all of this tax-deferred investment growth; the buildup of cash surrender value. However, when you save and invest in your 401(k) or an IRA, you get tax-deferred investment growth and a buildup of value, and you aren't paying fees to the insurance company. Plus, you have control over how the money is invested. Until you are maxing out on those tax-deferred savings vehicles, you don't need to pay extra in life insurance premiums to create savings.

The other downside is that if things get financially tight—someone loses a job or you have some big expenses—you have the flexibility to cut back on savings (in a real pinch), but you have no flexibility to cut back on paying a life insurance premium. If you don't pay, you don't have insurance. A universal policy does have some flexibility, but you need a hefty CSV to allow that. Term premiums will be much lower than a permanent insurance premium, so this creates less of a cash flow burden.

Permanent insurance makes sense only when you are financially secure. Before deciding, you should evaluate it yourself and be skeptical (really, really skeptical) about the illustrations that show massive growth of CSVs. What are the return assumptions? What if rates go down? There is no situation in the investing world where everything is up all the time, so be very wary, ask a lot of questions, and if it seems too good to be true, it is.

How much do you need?

There are some rules of thumb to look at, but again, it depends. Here are a few things to consider:

- Who are you protecting with this insurance? If you are a single parent providing support for a two-year-old child, you will need a different amount than if you provide support for your 90-year-old grandmother.

- What do you expect the insurance proceeds to be used for? You want to have enough money to (1) pay off all debt, (2) fund college for all kids, and (3) provide support for the surviving spouse.

- Support for the surviving spouse opens up another set of questions: How much per year will the spouse need to survive, and for how long? Does the spouse currently work? Would s/he continue to work? Would you want to provide funds, say, for the stay-at-home spouse to get a college education if s/he doesn't have a degree?

- How much do you have in assets now that could be used to offset the need for insurance?

The more specifically you can answer these questions, the better you can estimate what type of insurance you need.

Here are a few big picture guidelines:

- **10 times your annual income:** Essentially, you can think of this as your surviving spouse's planning window. Your spouse has 10 years of your income covered so that s/he could keep things as they are while making a plan for what to do next.

- **25 times your annual income:** This rule of thumb is more geared toward creating a life-long annuity[21] such that the investment

---

21 Annuity: Investment product, frequently offered by an insurance company, which provides for a life-long income at a set amount. For example, in lieu of receiving the death benefit on an insurance policy, the company will offer the beneficiary the opportunity to get a set monthly income for life. Financial planners use this concept when discussing the rule-of-thumb that an investor can create a life-long annuity from an investment balance if less than 4 percent of the balance is withdrawn annually.

earnings will grow and add to the balance at a fast enough rate that you get 30 or more years of annual expenses. Also, the expectation is that expenses would drop as kids go out on their own so you can stretch the payout into retirement when social security kicks in.

- **4 percent rule:** Theoretically, if you only withdraw 4 percent or less of a portfolio's balance each year, the money should last forever . . . theoretically. So if you have insurance proceeds of $1 million, your surviving spouse could withdraw $40,000 per year to live on and do that until the end of his or her life.

Again, clearly define what you want life insurance to achieve, estimate what the death benefit needs to be, and then balance that against what you can afford. In terms of amount of death benefit, leaving something for your dependents is better than nothing. Even covering funeral expenses and providing a little nest egg will help.

Life Insurance Quotes and the Underwriting Process

You can get free quotes on the web very quickly. Intelliquote.com provides multiple quotes from different companies, but you have to put in your name and phone number as well as your date of birth, tobacco use (matters a lot in terms of pricing), health status (or maybe height and weight depending on the company), term (start with 30 years), and death benefit.

Once you pick a company, you will fill out the application and then go through underwriting. This is the process that the insurance company uses to evaluate you and understand the risk they are assuming. The application asks health and lifestyle questions, then you have to have a mini-physical (usually) where someone comes to your house, weighs you, draws blood, takes a urine sample, and asks you similar health history questions as you answered on the app. Giving false information on an insurance application is fraud and can void benefits, so fess up on your real weight because someone with a scale is coming soon! Also, your quoted rate ("very good health") can change once the company looks at your blood work, health history, and family history. Going down a rate class will make the rate go up, obviously, and for some conditions you may have to go to a company that specializes in writing policies for "substandard" applicants. Translate that to "high premiums."

Health Insurance – See Chapter 2

Disability

Group disability was mentioned in Chapter 2. If you are self-employed, you need an individual disability policy, so there are a few more considerations.

The definition of disability is an important aspect of the policy. The social security definition is very narrow in that if you can do any kind of work making any kind of income, you will not be considered disabled. This could cause quite a drop in income if you go from being a brain surgeon to being a bagger at the grocery store, but for social security disability benefits, you are not disabled. This is obviously inadequate for most people. An individual disability policy can be based on own occupation (most expensive) to some modified version. It is important to understand the definitions in any policy you buy.

- Total disability means you cannot perform any of the major functions of your own occupation.
- Modified own occupation is when you can perform some of the major functions of your own occupation. In this definition, if you are able to resume work in another occupation for which you are educated or trained by virtue of your first occupation, you may cease benefits upon working in that occupation. For example, the brain surgeon becomes a medical school professor due to his inability to perform surgery because of the disability.
- Partial disability means you can perform some of the duties of your own occupation, but not all of them, so you may receive a partial benefit.
- Residual disability would occur in the event that you are able to work in some capacity, but not in your own occupation. You would

be paid the difference between your pre-disability income and your new income.

- **Benefit:** The benefit will be stated as a percentage of your monthly income up to a maximum amount. The premiums for disability insurance are not deductible, but the benefit received is not taxable income, so getting 67 percent of your monthly income as a benefit is probably about what your take-home pay would be after you consider payroll taxes and federal and state income tax withholding. The higher the percentage of income, the higher the premium. You cannot usually exceed 70 percent of monthly income.

- **Riders:** These are add-on specialty items within any policy that give better coverage than the basic policy but, of course, carry an add-on cost. There are some special riders for disability policies:

  - **Waiver of premium:** This allows you to stop paying premiums once you begin receiving benefits.

  - **Automatic benefit increases:** This rider provides for cost-of-living adjustments (COLA) to the benefit over time. Note that your benefit is a percentage of your monthly income up to a benefit maximum, which is determined when you write the policy. If you want to add to that base amount, you need this rider. This will only adjust based on inflation though, not on increases in your earnings over time.

Disability policies are really expensive. You have to weigh the cost against the possibility that you could become permanently and totally disabled and unable to work at all either due to accident or illness. Work through an agent and come up with a monthly amount that you can afford and work backwards to see what you can get for that amount of premium. It won't be the Cadillac policy, but it could buy you some time after a disability to get your new plan in place.

Here are some other options:

- **Your own savings.** If you become disabled, you are able to take money out of IRAs or other retirement accounts at no penalty, although you will pay income tax on your withdrawals.

- **A working spouse.** If you set up your household budget such that you can live on one income, then a disability would not totally devastate your family, but changes in your lifestyle would have to be made. Who would take care of the disabled spouse while the other one works? This is where long-term care insurance would be great. Unfortunately, most young people don't have it.

- **Credit life insurance.** This is a type of policy offered by mortgage companies which pays off the mortgage in the event of death, or makes the mortgage payment in the event of disability. It is usually inexpensive in terms of total dollars of monthly expense, but is expensive in terms of the premium relative to the benefit (as compared to term life insurance for example). However, if you cannot afford disability, this may be an option to at least ensure that the mortgage gets paid until you can figure out a new plan. If it only provides a death benefit and not a disability benefit, you should compare it to a term life policy, as you may get more benefit for the same cost with term life if you are young and healthy.

- **Social security disability.** Part of your payroll taxes go toward this benefit. It is a very restrictive definition, hard to get approved (hence, all of the TV ads from attorneys offering to help you get your social security benefit), and doesn't pay that much of a monthly benefit. Again, it's better than nothing, but you really can't qualify unless you can do nothing to earn a living—nothing.

- **Association or affiliation policies.** If you are a member of a professional organization (AICPA for accountants for example) or other group, check to see if they have insurance for their members. It may be worth the annual dues to pick up some kind of benefit through them.

The important thing is to create a plan around the issue of disability. The risk may be small, but the impact can be devastating.

Property and Casualty (P&C)

Renter's insurance:
- This is for you if you don't own the home that you live in but rent the living space from the owner.

- In insurance language, this is HO-4 and covers losses to your belongings from 16 different types of perils: fire or lightning, windstorm or hail, explosion, riot or civil commotion, damage from aircraft, damage from vehicles, smoke, vandalism, theft, volcanic eruption, falling objects, weight of ice, snow, or sleet, water from plumbing, heating, air conditioning, appliances or sprinkling system, plus three more involving explosion, freezing, or electric damage from household systems.

- Floods and earthquakes are not covered unless by a separate policy or rider, nor are damages due to hurricane winds, which also require a separate rider.

- You will need a separate rider for jewelry, computer, or other electronics that are very valuable and beyond what the average person would have.

- You should have an inventory of your belongings (or at least video each room so you see the basics of what you have). Go to www.knowyourstuff.org to set up an account free from the Insurance Information Institute.

- Most policies include coverage for liability, so if someone is injured or otherwise damaged because of your actions and sues you, you are covered up to the policy limits and subject to a deductible. This includes legal costs to defend you. Minimum liability coverages vary depending on the policy, so make sure you at least have your net worth covered.

- If you cannot live in your home, there is typically coverage for additional living expenses while your home is being repaired and is unlivable.

- Get the highest deductible you can afford in order to keep the premium lower.

- This is a must-have and many apartments require proof of renter's insurance in order to rent apartments. If you are living in a home (someone rents you a room), your belongings likely are not covered by the owner's homeowner's policy, so you should get a basic renter's policy. Search online and compare prices making sure to compare apples to apples in terms of coverages, deductibles, limits, exclusions, etc.

You may get a discount by using the same company that insures your car. There are also discounts for security systems, so ask your agent.

Homeowner's insurance:

- HO-2 is a broad homeowner's policy and covers the 16 perils identified above on renter's policies. In this case, those perils apply to the home itself as well as the contents.

- HO-3 is a special form policy and covers the home against all perils except those excluded by the policy. The contents are covered against perils named in the policy.

- HO-5 is a premier policy for newer, high-end homes that are well-maintained.

- HO-6 is for condos, and covers "walls in" since the actual structure is covered by the owner's association insurance policy.

- HO-8 is for older homes and may only cover repair costs or actual value since the replacement value may be very expensive.

Important considerations:

- Replacement value: you need to have your home rebuilt for whatever it costs.

- Understand what is NOT covered by your policy and consider if you need flood, earthquake, or hurricane coverage.

- Understand if and when you need a rider for valuables that may not be covered under the flat "contents" section.

- Consider the highest deductible that you could manage in order to save on premiums.

- Consider videotaping the inside of your house to document the contents or use www.knowyourstuff.org to complete your home inventory.

Commercial property insurance:

This is a very specialized area, so seek help from an experienced agent who handles this type of insurance.

Automobile insurance:

This is a must-have and most states require you to have coverage in order to even register a car in the state. Note that motorcycle coverage must be purchased separately. While the covered autos are those named in the policy, the people named as being insured are also covered when driving a non-owned auto (you borrow your friend's car). There are a number of components to an auto policy:

- **Uninsured/underinsured motorist** provides for payment by your insurance company for damages or injuries caused by another motorist who is either uninsured or underinsured, meaning that they have some insurance but not enough to compensate you for your losses. This is critical and most states require it.

- **Liability** covers both physical property and medical payments. (1) Physical property damage coverage provides repair to any property damaged by you as a result of an auto accident. For example, you run off the road and crash through someone's fence. (2) Medical payment coverage (bodily injury) provides for payments for medical expenses for covered persons, which is anyone riding in an insured vehicle, plus pedestrians or bicyclists injured as a result of the insured vehicle.

- **Collision** covers the cost of repairing your auto or providing actual cash value if it is totaled. This will not replace your car if it is totaled, but will give you the value of it. There may be a rider for a new car replacement. The coverage limit is the actual cash value of your car.

- **Comprehensive** (also called "other than collision") covers any kind of damage to your car from most anything: fire, theft, hail, animals, etc. Only get this if you have a new car, a leased car, or when your car still has a high value. The coverage limit is the actual cash value of your car.

- **Rental car coverage** provides up to a set amount per day if you have to rent a car while your car is being repaired or replaced as a result of an accident. The cost per year is pretty low, so it's probably worth it.

- **Coverage minimums** vary by state, but most require that you have auto liability insurance to cover those "innocents" whom you harm. To find out your state's minimum coverage limits, go to www.insure.com.

- **Coverage limits:** Auto insurance liability limits have three parts: (1) the per-person limit, (2) the per-incident limit, and (3) the property damage limit. It is usually written like this: $100/$300/$50 with each number being in thousands, so in this example, the policy would provide $100,000 of liability coverage per person who has a bodily injury, up to a maximum of $300,000 of coverage for all persons total for each incident, and $50,000 of coverage for damage to property. In other words, if one person has a total injury of $150,000, this policy would only cover $100,000 of expenses, but if six people each had $50,000 of expenses, the policy would cover the expenses for all of them. Typically, the maximums on these liability coverages are $250/$500/$100. To get more liability coverage, you need to get an umbrella policy.

Umbrella coverage:

An umbrella policy is another layer of protection that sits on top of your home and auto policies to provide liability coverage in excess of the maximums in those policies. One to two times your net worth in liability coverage is recommended and you would get this policy through your home and auto insurance company. So, if your net worth is $1 million and you have $500,000 of per incident coverage on both your home and auto policy, and are involved in an accident where the plaintiff is suing you for $1.5 million, your $1 million of assets is at risk. If there is a judgment against you, you only have $500,000 of liability coverage, assuming no one else from that accident had a claim. If you have umbrella coverage, that policy will kick in when the home or auto policy taps out.

- Also included is the cost to defend these suits. The insurance company wants to see that you have at least a pre-set coverage on your home and auto policy in order to qualify for the umbrella. If your current coverages are less than this, your insurance company will make you increase those first (increasing the premium cost) and then will write the umbrella.

- Usually, your home and auto insurance company will write the umbrella policy. It is unusual to have the umbrella with a separate company. It is usually cheaper to bundle your home/auto/umbrella anyway.

Long-term care insurance:

This type of insurance pays for nursing home care or in-home care if you are unable to perform some or all of the "activities of daily living" (ADLs), which include using the bathroom, eating, dressing, bathing, etc. This type of insurance is typically purchased by people in their mid- to late-50s or early 60s. The earlier you buy the policy, the less the monthly premium will be, but the longer you pay premiums.

For younger adults, this may be an issue to discuss with your parents to see if they have it, as caring for elderly parents can be a major expense for people in their 20s and 30s who are working and raising their children. Having some benefit can ease the burden significantly. If this is important for your family situation, visit www.insideeldercare.com and review their information about long-term care insurance or talk to a qualified insurance agent. There are a lot of choices that impact the benefit and the premium including the daily benefit amount, the waiting period, inflation adjustments, benefit period, and costs covered (in-home care versus nursing home care). Ideally, you can talk with an agent who is able to get quotes from several companies so that you can compare.

Ask a lot of questions about the details, riders, etc. so you understand what is covered. If this is a policy for a parent, you may or may not be involved in some of this, but if your parents don't have a policy, don't have significant assets, and need care, you will be thrust into dealing with it. Better to ask some personal questions now and be armed with knowledge.

Getting a Quote

For some types of insurance like term life, it is easy to get a quote on an insurance company's website. For others like long-term care, you will need to contact an agent. If you don't know someone, ask your friends and family members for a referral. If they don't know anyone, research the insurance company, and their website will likely provide a directory of agents in your area.

Getting a quote is free and is not binding on either party. The quote is just an estimate until you have completed an application and gone through underwriting. Agents are used to providing quotes and should be able to do so quickly and easily. Review details and ask questions once you get the quote back. It is critical that you understand what is covered and what is not.

CHAPTER 8

Saving and Investing

In this chapter:

- Why Invest? The Power of Compounding
- Inflation
- How To Invest
- How To Pick Investments
- Transaction Costs and Commissions
- You Invested, Now What?
- Tax Implications of Investing
- Sell Methodology

You could fill libraries with all of the books written about investing. The good news is, you don't have to know everything about technical analysis and portfolio theory to be an investor. Obtain some basic knowledge and then, over time, build up experience. The best place to start is to examine your reasons for investing.

Why Invest? The Power of Compounding

To understand why investing should be part of your financial plan, you should understand the power of compounding and the impact of inflation.

Remember the amortization schedule shown in Chapter 5 when

examining how to pay off your debt? Think about this from the perspective of a lender:

- Suppose you loan someone $1,000 at 5 percent interest and they repay you over a year. You make $27.29 in interest. Fine, but what if you don't actually want to be repaid right now? You want to let the borrower use that money for a long time and pay you interest, which keeps getting added to the original principal you loaned them. This is called compound interest[22] because instead of getting interest payments every month, the interest payments are added to the principal, so you, the lender, get paid interest on the interest. This is how a basic savings account works: you are lending the bank money; they pay you interest every month which adds to the balance and then the interest is calculated on the higher balance. You, as a "lender" to the bank, get a return on your money.

Here's what that looks like:

Month	Balance	Interest earned	Interest + balance	Amount paid to investor	New balance
1	$1,000.00	$4.17	$1,004.17	$0.00	$1,004.17
2	$1,004.17	$4.18	$1,008.35	$0.00	$1,008.35
3	$1,008.35	$4.20	$1,012.55	$0.00	$1,012.55
4	$1,012.55	$4.22	$1,016.77	$0.00	$1,016.77
5	$1,016.77	$4.24	$1,021.01	$0.00	$1,021.01
6	$1,021.01	$4.25	$1,025.26	$0.00	$1,025.26
7	$1,025.26	$4.27	$1,029.53	$0.00	$1,029.53
8	$1,029.53	$4.29	$1,033.82	$0.00	$1,033.82
9	$1,033.82	$4.31	$1,038.13	$0.00	$1,038.13
10	$1,038.13	$4.33	$1,042.46	$0.00	$1,042.46
11	$1,042.46	$4.34	$1,046.80	$0.00	$1,046.80
12	$1,046.80	$4.36	$1,051.16	$0.00	$1,051.16

---

22 Compound interest: Interest payments which are added to the principal balance so that the next interest calculation is based on the new, higher principal. Traditional savings accounts have interest compounded.

See how the new balance includes the interest already earned? At the end of one year, you have earned $51.16 instead of $27.29. Now you see how interest on interest works and why it matters.

Consider what would happen with the same savings by adding just $25 every month:

Month	Balance	Interest earned	Interest + balance	Amount paid to investor	New balance	Additional savings
1	$1,000.00	$4.17	$1,004.17	$0.00	$1,004.17	$0.00
2	$1,029.17	$4.29	$1,033.45	$0.00	$1,033.45	$25.00
3	$1,058.45	$4.41	$1,062.87	$0.00	$1,062.87	$25.00
4	$1,087.87	$4.53	$1,092.40	$0.00	$1,092.40	$25.00
5	$1,117.40	$4.66	$1,122.05	$0.00	$1,122.05	$25.00
6	$1,147.05	$4.78	$1,151.83	$0.00	$1,151.83	$25.00
7	$1,176.83	$4.90	$1,181.74	$0.00	$1,181.74	$25.00
8	$1,206.74	$5.03	$1,211.76	$0.00	$1,211.76	$25.00
9	$1,236.76	$5.15	$1,241.92	$0.00	$1,241.92	$25.00
10	$1,266.92	$5.28	$1,272.20	$0.00	$1,272.20	$25.00
11	$1,297.20	$5.40	$1,302.60	$0.00	$1,302.60	$25.00
12	$1,327.60	$5.53	$1,333.13	$0.00	$1,333.13	$25.00

See how your interest grows each month as you add more principal?

After seven years, you would have $3,901.25 consisting of $3,075 of principal ($1,000 + 2,075 [7 x 12 x 25] – 25 since you didn't put in month one) and $826.25 of interest.

Here is what it looks like in the last month of year seven:

Month	Balance	Interest earned	Interest + balance	Amount paid to investor	New balance	Additional savings
84	$3,885	$16.19	$3,901.25	$0.00	$3,901.25	$25.00

Your monthly income is increasing, and that is just on $25 per month. The rate matters, though. Take a look at this view of year seven at 8 percent:

Month	Balance	Interest earned	Interest + balance	Amount paid to investor	New balance	Additional savings
84	$4,495	$29.97	$4,525.25	$0.00	$4,525.25	$25.00

Now at 0.5 percent (closer to a money market[23]):

Month	Balance	Interest earned	Interest + balance	Amount paid to investor	New balance	Additional savings
84	$3,146	$1.31	$3,147.34	$0.00	$3,147.34	$25.00

When examining compounding, both the rate and the length of time matter. As a young adult, you have a long time period to invest, so if you consistently add principal and keep compounding the interest, you could accumulate some sizable investment balances.

Inflation

Inflation is the rise in prices over time, typically with regard to consumer goods, food, and the like.

Back in the 1970s, gas cost 35 cents per gallon (hard to believe). Today, one gallon of gas is easily more than $3 per gallon. Compare the cost of most any other item or service from 40 years ago with the cost today, and you'll see how inflation plays a part in every aspect of life over time. This is called purchasing power.

---

23 Money Market: A type of mutual fund whose investment goal is liquidity and safety of principal. The goal of a money market fund is to maintain a $1 price and be essentially equivalent to cash, but pay a higher "dividend" than a savings account. In order to achieve this, the fund company invests in very stable bonds, such as Treasury issues, inter-bank loans, etc., which earns a bit more than a traditional savings account but is still safe and not volatile.

You need to keep your purchasing power the same in the future (at financial independence) as it is today. To do this, you have to invest your savings such that those dollars at least maintain their purchasing power over time. This gives you the opportunity to buy the same goods and services with those dollars in the future that you can buy today.

The bottom line is that you cannot bury your money in the backyard nor put it in a low-interest savings account and wake up in 40 years thinking that you can live the same lifestyle that you live today. That's why you must invest your money.

The price of goods is impacted by not only inflation, but also by supply and demand, the political climate (especially around gas), the economy in general, and how it impacts employment, among many other factors. Economists track inflation by defining a "basket of goods," and every year, they "go shopping" for this same basket of goods and see how much it costs. That gets compared to the prior year so they can calculate the change in the Consumer Price Index (CPI), a common way to measure inflation.

The compounding of inflation over time erodes the purchasing power of a dollar. To combat that, you must earn more than inflation every year so that your interest compounding beats the inflation compounding. That's another reason why you must invest—to beat inflation. You also hope to grow your assets, obviously, but you must grow them enough to cover inflation first and then to get additional purchasing power.

How To Invest

At the most basic level, you need an investment account. To get one, you can:

- Open a 401(k) or other retirement account through your employer's retirement plan.
- Go online to one of the brokerage sites and open an account (Schwab, TD Ameritrade, Fidelity, e*Trade, etc.).

- Go to a mutual fund company (Vanguard, T. Rowe Price, Invesco, etc.) online and open an account with them.
- Go to www.computershare.com and open an account to buy corporate stocks starting with small dollars (some as low as $50 to get started). These are direct stock purchase plans (DSPPs) or dividend reinvestment plans (DRIPs).

Types of Accounts

- **Individual:** Opening an individual, non-qualified account means that you, and you alone, own the account (individual), and it has no special tax benefits (non-qualified).
  - Qualified accounts are retirement accounts. Your 401(k) is qualified (by a section of the tax code (section 401(k)), meaning that the earnings on the account are not taxable until withdrawn. IRAs (individual retirement accounts) and Roth IRAs are also qualified.
- **Joint:** If you are married and both you and your spouse will own the account, you will open a joint account.
  - Usually for spouses, you open a joint tenants with right of survivorship account (JTWRS). As it sounds, JTWRS accounts pass by law to the surviving account owner (right of survivorship) in the event of the death of the other account owner (spouses co-owning accounts is the typical example.)
  - A tenants in common (TIC) account means that each person owns his/her share of the account which passes, at their death, via the terms of their will.

Once you have an account, you will need to deposit some money, access your account online, and select the investment(s) you want to buy. The brokerage houses (and the internet) make it pretty easy now.

Types of Investments

- **Stock:** Companies issue stock to the public via an IPO (initial public offering) to raise money. After that offering of stock, investors who want to sell their shares do so on a stock exchange: New York

Stock Exchange (NYSE) or NASDAQ. You can be a buyer or a seller if you have a brokerage account (Schwab, TD Ameritrade, etc.). A few pros and cons to consider are:

- You don't have to think about what stock exchange the stock trades on as the brokerage house manages all of that behind the scenes. You just click "buy" and next thing you know the shares show up in your account.

- There may still be some issues with restrictions on the quantity of stock you can buy. Round lots are 100 shares, so you may need a decent amount of money to buy a high-priced stock if it must be purchased in round lots; however, many round lot restrictions have been eliminated in the online brokerage world.

- You can buy shares in small quantities using www.computer-share.com which manages the DSPPs and DRIPs for many U.S. companies that offer such plans. They let you buy small amounts of their stock, usually if you have set up an automatic monthly deposit into the account.

- **Bonds:** This debt instrument issued by a company, government, government agency (Sallie Mae, Freddie Mac, etc.), or utility raises money to fund their projects. Bonds have a term (period of time until repayment), an interest rate, and a set period for interest payments (monthly, quarterly, semi-annually, or annually).

- **Mutual Funds:** Mutual funds have a fund manager who sets the fund objective (health care growth stocks or high tech or alternative energy, for example), and then buys corporate stocks or other investments (bonds, options, futures, currencies) that meet the fund objective. Because mutual funds are a group of investments, the downfall of a single company doesn't wipe you out.

  - **Open-end funds:** With these mutual funds the purchase and sale of the fund is handled between the investor and the fund company (can be through a brokerage account though), and the fund simply issues more shares if demand is high. They are priced daily based on the net asset value (NAV) of the underlying holdings within the fund. If the fund gets too large, the fund may close to new investors.

- **Closed-end funds:** These are mutual funds where the fund company issues a fixed number of shares for sale to the public in an IPO similar to a stock issue. They are then traded (and priced) based on supply and demand rather than NAV.

- **Exchange traded funds (ETFs):** These mutual funds trade like stocks on an exchange. They usually track an index (say the S&P 500) or a commodity or other "basket of assets." The expenses are usually lower for these funds than other mutual funds.

- **Index funds:** These mutual funds mimic a particular index, such as the Dow Jones Industrials or the Wilshire Total Market Index. They are typically low cost and are meant to let you invest in the index without actually having to buy every stock that makes up the index.

Classification of Mutual Funds

There are stock funds and bond funds. There are funds that focus on a particular market segment, such as health care or high tech, and funds that are geared toward growth or income. If you can think of a classification or category, there is probably a mutual fund focused on it. Just about every investing objective can be covered through a mutual fund.

Investment Considerations

The three critical factors to consider when answering this question are:

- How much time do you have before you need access to the investment proceeds? This is called the time horizon. The longer the time horizon, the more risk you can take with the investment (equities). The shorter the time horizon, the more conservative you want to be (guaranteed interest, bonds).

- What is your investment objective? If you need to purchase a house in five years, for example, safety of your principal is very important. On the other hand, if you are investing to create financial independence in 50 years, you might select very different types of investments than when you are saving for a specific purchase or event, because you can weather more ups and downs in the market. Consider whether you have a growth objective or an income objective. For growth, you want appreciation of the investment over time. For income, you want the investment to give you cash flow on a periodic basis (like paying you interest or dividends).

- What is your risk tolerance? Risk is tied to the previous two factors: objective and time horizon. The bigger the swings in highs and lows of the stock price over the short term, the more volatile the investment is, and generally the more risk it carries.

Risk tolerance is also emotional, to an extent. Here is where you need to examine your tolerance for risk. Ask yourself, "If I lost 25 percent to 40 percent of this investment in the short term would I be able to continue adding money to it knowing that over the long term, it will recover and the investment could grow?" You must have that attitude in order to take on the volatility of equities. If the answer is "no" (for example, if this money is for a down payment on a house in a year), you should not invest that money in equities. Your risk tolerance for that pot of money is too low for equities.

The key to managing your risk tolerance is to be very clear about what this investment is for (emergency savings, down payment on a house, college education for your 1-year-old, or financial independence). You should also understand that over long periods of time, the intermittent highs and lows are less of an issue allowing you to see the overall upward trend in the market. So, in the long term, take on the risk of equities; in the short term, don't. Once you get that in place, do your best to manage your emotions. When the market goes up 25 percent in a year, that's nice. When it goes down 25 percent in a day, hold tight and know that it will come back up.

How do you know how much risk an investment has?

Investing involves a spectrum of risk, from very conservative (a bank deposit) to very aggressive (junk bonds and speculative investments). You have to take on some risk to earn enough interest to beat inflation and to get a better return on your investments. Higher risk means higher potential return because you also have potential to lose the money. Low risk, low return just doesn't work for long-term purchasing power.

Low risk ⟶	High risk
Money market	Start-ups
Bank savings	Junk bonds
CDs	Roulette wheel
U.S. Treasury issues	

Every other kind of asset (investment) falls somewhere between the two extremes. Figure 1 is a graph from www.finance.yahoo.com that shows what volatility looks like for some asset classes. Notice how the prices fluctuate in the short-term but seem to smooth out over very long time periods.

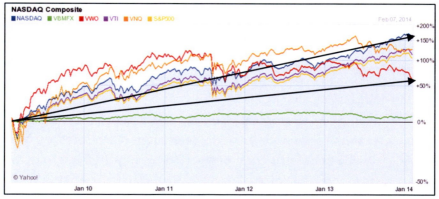

Figure 1

See how all of the lines at the top are little roller coasters? Up, down, up, down. That is volatility. The black straight line demonstrates that, despite all of the drama of daily volatility, over the last five years, the market has gone up; it just covered a lot of ground in between. That's why your time frame is so critical. Figure 2 shows a longer time frame:

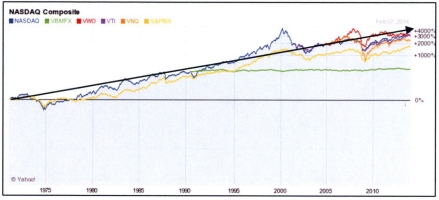

Figure 2

Viewing the same investments since 1970 illustrates that the drama of the volatility gets smoothed out. That is what you have to think about when you invest—the long upward climb that the market takes. You can't worry about the little dips and the intermediate peaks and valleys along the way. Keep your eye on the summit and ignore the swings in the middle.

The other thing to notice is the correlation, or the tendency for investments to move in the same direction at the same time. Notice in Figure 3 how all the lines (except green) mirror each other, but not to the same extreme and not at exactly the same time, but close.

Figure 3

As one drops, they all seem to drop. That means that they are positively correlated. When you have positive correlation, you aren't truly diversified. In other words, your investments are all on the same roller coaster. You can be diversified across countries, industries, or individual companies, but if everything is positively correlated, it isn't helping to reduce the volatility of your investment portfolio. Ideally, you want some investments that are negatively correlated so that if one is going down, the other goes up. That levels out the impact on the total portfolio.

Asset Classes

Investment managers group stocks or mutual funds into asset classes to help them understand the risk and return potential of various investments. The big three asset classes—U.S. equities, international equities, and bonds—are what most people use to diversify (split money up among investment segments).

Among the big three, there are different sub-classes within the asset class:

1. U.S. equities
   - Large cap (capitalization—the total value of their outstanding stock). These can be broken into mega-cap, large cap, and mid-cap.
   - Small cap
2. International equities
   - General international (businesses in developed countries, primarily countries in Europe and Asia)
   - Emerging markets (businesses in developing countries like those in Brazil and South Korea)
3. Bonds
   - By type: U.S. bonds, international bonds, emerging markets bonds
   - By duration (time frame): Long-term, short-term
   - By credit quality: AAA to junk
   - By taxability: Taxable bonds versus tax-exempt bonds

U.S. Equities

- **Large caps (market capitalization[24]):** These are the established companies like McDonald's, Coke, and IBM that tend to be more stable. Many pay dividends, as they don't need all their cash to invest back into the business.

- **Small caps:** These may be newer companies or established companies that have remained small as compared to the large cap companies. They may have an innovative product or technology, but they might go bust for a number of reasons, ranging from lack of operating capital to ineffective management.

International Equities

- General international are companies in already developed countries.

---

24 Market capitalization or "market cap" is the total number of outstanding shares of stock multiplied by the price of the stock.

- Emerging markets focus on companies in developing countries. These stocks are generally high risk, but are definitely a good place to be invested when you have a 40- to 50-year time frame, as prospects for growth are greater outside the United States.

Bonds

When you put your money in a deposit account (essentially a guaranteed interest scenario), you receive an interest payment because the financial institution takes your money and lends it to others, like other banks and AAA-rated institutions that need short-term loans. It's very safe and secure. For letting them use your money, they pay you interest. The interest rate is pretty low because there is essentially no risk of loss to the investor because regular bank deposits and money markets are FDIC-insured in case something goes wrong with the bank.

The U.S. government is the most credit-worthy entity and is actually backing up the banks. The government needs to borrow money daily so it issues various types of interest-bearing debt:

- T-bills (Treasury bills) are very liquid (easily converted to cash) instruments that mature in a year or less
- T-notes mature in one to 10 years
- T-bonds are long-term issues that mature in more than 10 years

These are (in 2014), the "risk-free" investments, so they pay rock-bottom interest rates. In the same way creditors consider your payment history when deciding if you are credit-worthy, you should also consider a company or entity you are lending money to or investing in. Ask yourself if they can pay you back in addition to paying you interest. In the case of the U.S. government, the answer is yes, so there is no premium added to the rate because of credit risk (the risk that they can't repay).

State and local governments also issue bonds, typically at more risk. These local governments can't get more money without raising taxes, and that requires voter buy-in. Some cities have come close to bankruptcy, so when you look at lending to them (buying their bonds), you should expect a better return than what you would get in a risk-free investment. You want to get compensated for taking on more risk. However, the interest on these is exempt from federal income taxes so that has the opposite impact; they can pay lower rates than say a corporate bond that has taxable interest.

You also can buy corporate bonds issued by a corporation like Home Depot or Walmart. There isn't much of a risk-premium on their debt, so the return will likely be low.

Junk bonds are issued by companies that are so credit-UNworthy that the bond is more like a bet. These might be companies trying to come out of bankruptcy or that have experienced major cash flow problems. The rates on these bonds are high because there is a high risk of default; therefore, these bonds can be quite a gamble. However, if the company survives, the return can be quite high.

Bond prices are driven by interest rates. Since interest rates in the United States have been low for a long time, there hasn't been much movement in the bond world. However, as interest rates increase, bond prices will decrease.

Example: You purchase a 10-year bond paying 2 percent from an AAA-rated company. This is a low credit risk. Compared to a money market, 2 percent is decent, so you go for it. You earn interest annually, and in year two, interest rates go up dramatically so that new bonds issued by this company are paying 4 percent. If you have to sell your bond, who would want to buy a 2 percent bond when they can get a 4 percent bond? In order to sell your bond, you will have to decrease the price. Even if you don't have to sell it, you aren't very happy that your $1,000 bond is earning only 2 percent when you could be getting 4 percent. That is the risk with buying a bond, and it is called interest rate risk—the risk that the rate will increase after you buy the bond.

How To Pick Investments

Researching the economy, markets, asset classes, individual stocks, individual bonds, etc., is time consuming. So here is the quick and easy approach to deciding which investment to choose:

- Understand what asset allocation you are looking for. In other words, what asset classes will you invest in and what percentage of your total portfolio will you put in each one?
  - Look on your brokerage or 401(k) website and search for "growth allocation." You will likely find their recommendation of what a growth portfolio would look like. Here is what TD Ameritrade's website shows for conservative and aggressive growth:

	Conservative	Aggressive
U.S. equities	14%	51%
International equities	4%	27%
Domestic bonds	69%	7%
International bonds	8%	3%
Specialty	4%	11%
Cash	1%	1%

They also show moderate, moderate growth, and growth allocations as other options.

For money in a 401(k) or an IRA that you have earmarked for financial independence, you are looking for growth, so you want to select an investment option in the growth to a high-growth or even aggressive allocation, depending on your specific objectives and risk tolerance.

"Growth" stocks or mutual funds are those where the objective is to see the share value increase but probably not to see the companies pay a lot of dividends. "Value" stocks or mutual funds are those where the manager is looking for a "deal" (a company whose stock is perceived to be undervalued) and so the price appreciation is more the result of catching up. They are likely to pay dividends which adds to the return.

See Figure 4 where this website further breaks down each of these categories into segments within each asset class.

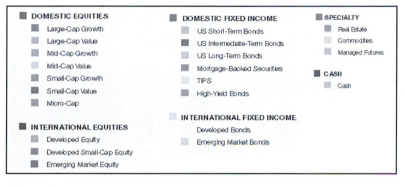

Figure 4

This is a lot to look at. And it's even more confusing to make stock or fund picks based on all of those elements, especially if you are just getting started and you don't have a lot of money yet. When searching for allocation ideas, you will see break-downs like this one. When you have more money accumulated and want to get a little fancier, you can break down your asset classes further. For now, keep it simple.

- Look at the big three in terms of your asset classes (U.S. equities, international equities, and bonds). You can have a solid, diversified investment portfolio by picking only three funds to invest in. That means you are only looking to pick three investments. Look at ETFs (exchange traded funds), as these are low cost and can give you broad coverage of the asset class. Hopefully you will see the option for commission-free ETFs. Consider these points:
  - Index funds will give you the whole index, so if you want to invest in the S&P 500 as your U.S. equity asset class, look for an S&P 500 index fund.

- You can also look to invest in a "total stock market" for U.S. equities or an "all world" mutual fund for your international equities. Bond funds have the same type of "all world" or "all corporate" orientation, as well as funds geared toward short-term or long-term bonds.

- The TD Ameritrade site gives you the expense ratio as well. Every fund charges fees. The expenses come off the top before the fund calculates its returns. Select funds that have a lower expense ratio. Note that specialty funds and actively managed funds (REITS, precious metals, natural resources, and the like) will have higher expense ratios than an index fund.

- There might also be trading fees or commissions. These are fees charged by the broker.

- When you don't understand something, visit investopedia.com for great definitions and commentary about investing terms.

- Many brokerage sites have a chat feature and a mountain of information about investing to help with your research in this area.

- The fund (or stock issuer) is required to provide a prospectus, a written explanation to investors about important details of the fund (or stock). Items like the fund objective, cost of the fund, other charges, and risks are in the prospectus. Pull up the prospectus for a couple of funds to get an idea about what they contain. It is always a great idea to read the prospectus before you invest, even if all you do is look at the objective, risk, and the fees.

- Many sites will give you a Morningstar rating. Morningstar is a research organization that gathers and reports data, and has investment analysts out the wazoo.

As a quick and easy way to check out the volatility (risk) of your fund go to www.finance.yahoo.com and type in the ticker symbol[25]. You will

---

25 Ticker symbol: Symbol used by a stock exchange to identify a company or mutual fund.

get a lot of information about the stock or mutual fund you're researching, including the name of the fund, the quote, the return, a chart showing the price over time, and various links to access more information. The chart gives you a visual of what the price history has been over time. You can customize the chart by selecting a time frame as well as add other ticker symbols or indices to compare that fund to.

> **Note:** This example is for educational purposes only, and should not be construed as investment advice. What is appropriate for you may not be appropriate for someone else, even at the same age, income level, or asset level, so you should always evaluate your own situation, objectives, and risk tolerance before making investment decisions.

This is only an example, and is in no way a recommendation of a specific brokerage site or any specific funds. Always review the fund prospectus and consider its investment objectives, risks, and fees prior to investing. The TD Ameritrade site is being used only as an example to demonstrate an easy process for gathering information about investment options.

Suppose you have $10,000 in an IRA. If you used the TD Ameritrade recommendation for an aggressive allocation, that portfolio of $10,000 would be invested as follows:

Asset Class	Percentage	Amount
U.S. equities	51%	$5,100
International	27%	$2,700
Bonds	10%	$1,000
Specialty	11%	$1,100
Cash	1%	$100

Examine the commission-free ETF funds available on the TD Ameritrade site. Again, this site is used only as an example, not as a recommendation.

U.S. Equities

There are tabs for the various asset classes. Under the Equities tab, there are many choices. A quick sort by "Gross Expense Ratio" turns up the SPDR Dow Jones Global Real Estate ETF has expenses of 0.50 percent. This specialty fund is more expensive to run so that makes sense. You might consider that under the "specialty" category later on.

> **Note**: Expense ratio is not the only thing or even necessarily the most important thing when picking a fund; however, for picking these big "cover the whole asset class" funds, this example looks at index funds, so the index is what it is. The differentiator will be cost, for the most part. As you get into actively managed funds, you probably don't want the bargain basement fund!

The least expensive fund is the Vanguard Total Stock Market ETF at 0.05 percent. Total stock market would be about as diversified as you could get within this asset class. Morningstar calls it a "Large Blend" which means large cap stocks and a blend between growth and value.

Next, click the little P next to the fund name and see the prospectus. The prospectus for these type funds indicates the following:

- **Investment Objective**

  "The Fund seeks to track the performance of a benchmark index that measures the investment return of the overall stock market." It then goes into detail about what makes up that 0.05 percent fee, gives an example, talks about portfolio turnover (their own buying and selling of stocks within the fund), and then details the primary investment strategy.

- **Risk**

  The next section is about risks, which is important to understand. It then talks about the historic returns of the fund, and gives details about who is managing the fund. The ticker is VTI, so go to www.finance.yahoo.com and put it in to the chart. You'll get the easy option to also track the S&P500, NASDAQ, and the Dow. Click those boxes and see in Figure 5 how this equity compares in the short term.

Figure 5

They are all riding the same ride, that's for sure. Next, you will want to select "max" as the range to get an idea of the long-term performance. Figure 6 shows the longer-term view.

Figure 6

The fund has only been around since 2002, which is fine. A lot of the ETFs and index funds aren't very old. This fund is a bumpy ride for sure. You can see that 2009 was the last big crash. That was the start of the great recession, but here's the critical thing to understand by this picture: the market had a "bad day" back in late 2008/2009, but it came back up; it still grew from there.

The market will have more bad days. Investing in this fund means that on those days, you may not want to look at your losses, but even if you do, you have to push your emotions out of the way and decide,

- "I want to buy more."
- "These aren't real losses as long as I don't sell."
- "This is a great sale!"

Note: If an investor owned this stock prior to the 2008/2009 crash, and didn't sell, s/he would be further ahead now than they were in late 2007 before the crash.

International Equities

Going through the same process for the international category, you see in Figure 7 the funds that have the lowest expense ratio:

Equity 32 Funds	Sector 2 Funds	Bond 33 Funds	International 31 Funds		Commodity 3 Funds	

Symbol	Prospectus	Fund	Today's Change	Last	▼ Gross Expense Ratio	Rating	Morningstar Category
VEA	P	Vanguard FTSE Developed Markets ETF	+0.18 (+0.44%)	$41.23	0.10%	★★★	Foreign Large Blend
VGK	P	Vanguard FTSE Europe ETF	+0.27 (+0.46%)	$59.15	0.12%	★★★	Europe Stock
VEU	P	Vanguard FTSE All-World ex-US ETF	+0.23 (+0.46%)	$49.81	0.15%	★★★	Foreign Large Blend
VWO	P	Vanguard FTSE Emerging Markets ETF	+0.47 (+1.22%)	$39.10	0.18%	★★★	Diversified Emerging Mkts
VT	P	Vanguard Total World Stock Index ETF	+0.29 (+0.49%)	$58.89	0.19%	★★★	World Stock

Figure 7

The least expensive fund is only covering developed markets so you would either miss out on emerging markets or have to pick another fund. You decide on just one fund, so moving down the list, you see the next one is only Europe (getting narrower). The next one is Vanguard FTSE All-World ex-United States (no U.S. companies). That sounds pretty broad, and it eliminates U.S. companies so you would not get any crossover with your U.S. equities asset class. The Morningstar category is Foreign Large Blend so you are looking at big companies, both growth and value.

Select that one. You can select other funds and then show the chart for all of them at once.

Bonds

Here, begin with lowest expense ratio.

There are 33 different bond ETFs that are commission-free. Look first at the Morningstar category; most are intermediate-term. That's OK; however, when interest rates are low, you want to avoid a long-term fund because when rates do go up, bond prices go down. In low rate environments, stay shorter-term or use an actively managed fund. When interest rates are high, look at longer-term. Let's chart a few of these so you can see the impact. Figure 8 shows a few bond funds for the year ended Feb 2014.

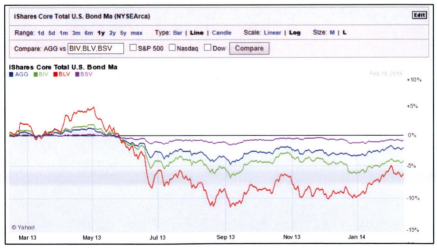

Figure 8

Bond funds didn't do well in 2013. Interest rates went up in mid-2013 so prices went down. Leading the losers, in red, was that long-term bond fund. The next worst, in green, was the intermediate bond fund. Next worse, in blue, was the total U.S. bond fund (also an intermediate range fund) and then leading the pack (but still negative) was the short-term fund in purple.

Figure 9 provides the longer-term view:

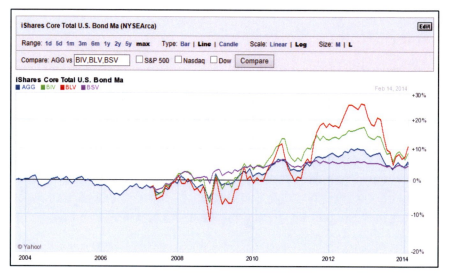

Figure 9

So what does this tell you about the volatility of red versus purple? The short-term is going to be less volatile so keep that in mind as you select your bond fund.

Specialty

For specialty, the TD Ameritrade site shows two "sector" funds which are both real estate (any time you see REIT—real estate investment trust—you know it is real estate) and three commodity funds (commodities are goods that can't be differentiated by who produced them—agricultural products, oil, precious metals—they are all the same). Commodities are "real assets" in that you can touch and feel an actual bushel of wheat or barrel of oil or ounce of gold.

Figure 10 shows the REITs:

Commission-Free ETF List

Category	Fund Family	Market Cap	All Funds		🔻 Download Commission-Free ETF List

Equity 32 Funds	Sector 2 Funds	Bond 33 Funds	International 31 Funds	Commodity 3 Funds

Symbol ▾	Prospectus	Fund	Today's Change	Last	Gross Expense Ratio	Rating	Morningstar Category
RWR	P	SPDR Dow Jones REIT ETF	+0.26 (+0.34%)	$76.65	0.25%	★★	Real Estate
VNQ	P	Vanguard REIT Index ETF	+0.27 (+0.39%)	$69.39	0.10%	★★★	Real Estate

Figure 10

Figure 11 shows the commodities funds:

Category	Fund Family	Market Cap	All Funds		🔻 Download Commission-Free ETF List

Equity 32 Funds	Sector 2 Funds	Bond 33 Funds	International 31 Funds	Commodity 3 Funds

Symbol ▾	Prospectus	Fund	Today's Change	Last	Gross Expense Ratio	Rating	Morningstar Category
DBC	P	PowerShares DB Commodity Index Tracking Trust	+0.09 (+0.35%)	$25.78	0.85%	★★★	Commodities Broad Basket
DBO	P	PowerShares DB Oil Trust	+0.05 (+0.18%)	$28.07	0.75%	Not Rated	Commodities Energy
DJP	P	iPath Dow Jones-UBS Commodity Index Total Return ETN	+0.13 (+0.34%)	$38.28	0.75%	★★★	Commodities Broad Basket

Figure 11

Chart these now so you can see the real deal with these funds (Figure 12):

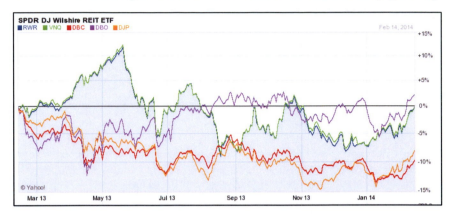

Figure 12

Now you can see what volatility is. You can see why a conservative portfolio would only have 4 percent of its money here. Even the aggressive only has 11 percent because it is quite a ride in the short-term. The two REITs are in blue and green and they are so correlated that they're hard to differentiate. Purple is oil and the orange and red are "commodities broad basket" so a large cross-section of the commodities market.

Now, look to Figure 13 for the long-term view:

Figure 13

Again, the long view is much smoother but oil (purple) hit its high in late 2008 and real estate (green) hit its bottom in 2009. Between all of these, it appears the real estate fund is the best option. VNQ has the lower expense ratio, and Vanguard is solid, so go with that one for this example.

Here is your allocation:

- U.S. – VTI (blue) $5,100

- International – VEU (green) $2,700

- Bond – BSV (purple) $1,000

- Specialty – VNQ (red) $1,100

Figure 14

Figure 14 shows how this portfolio would have performed over time if you had it back in 2004. Look at that little purple bond fund holding up the portfolio back in 2009 when all asset classes went off a cliff!

What do you know about this portfolio? You know that all funds except the bonds are positively correlated over this time frame; they are all moving in the same direction at roughly the same time. You know that you can expect to see your asset balance go up and down a lot, especially among those three asset classes. You also see that over a long time period you should expect an overall upward climb.

There was a lot of information in that example, and hopefully you can see that getting started with investing isn't that hard. The example stuck with commission-free ETFs, picked funds in just four asset classes, and started by looking at low expense index funds. You can delve much deeper into the selection and you can subdivide the asset classes further, but at the most basic level, you can keep it very reasonable and narrow the choices considerably. Once your investment balances start to increase, you can delve more deeply or seek outside advice from someone who spends their day doing investment analysis, but for now, get your retirement money invested in something besides a money market fund.

I was so, so, so intimidated by the whole idea of investing back when I started working that I did nothing—I saved some money but didn't invest it well. I hope this will help you to dip your toes in to the investing pool. The water is great. Just know that there will be waves, and that's OK!

Transaction Costs and Commissions

There are several kinds of costs related to investing. Read all of the information about fees so you know exactly what your trade will cost before you place it.

- **Expense ratio of the mutual fund:** This cost of administering the mutual fund comes off the top, before the fund reports its returns. The cost is disclosed in the prospectus.
  - **Purchase or redemption fee:** Some mutual funds charge this fee upon the purchase or sale of shares.
  - **Load fees of the mutual fund:** These are the commissions paid upon either the purchase of shares (front-end load) or sale of shares (back-end load or deferred sales charge).
- **Brokerage fees or commissions:** These fees are charged by the broker and should be clearly shown on the website.

- There may be different fees for internet trades (cheapest), voice response phone trades (expensive compared to internet), and broker-assisted trades (these are expensive).

- There can be a fee for holding ETFs short-term. Check the details on the broker's website.

These fees can be significant when making small trades, so get into your funds and hold on for the long haul. If you want to do a lot of trading, consider the impact of these fees as they can eat up your profits quickly.

You Invested, Now What?

Now, you keep adding to it. Set up an automated investment plan, which allows you to deposit funds on a specified date, making the process easy. If this isn't an option for you, then buy more shares periodically as cash builds up in your account. Again, consider transaction costs.

Over time, that original allocation will get skewed. Keeping an eye on your portfolio lets you know when to rebalance and get the allocation closer to your target. This helps you stay diversified, stay within the allocation, and helps you buy low and sell high.

Here is a chart to show you how this works. You can create something similar in Excel:

Account balance:	$15,000				
	Target Allocation		Actual Balances	Difference: buy or (sell)	Under (over) weight
U.S. equities	51%	$7,650	$6,000	$1,650	22%
International	27%	$4,050	$5,500	($1,450)	(36%)
Bonds	10%	$1,500	$1,450	$50	3%
Specialty	11%	$1,650	$1,300	$350	21%
Cash	1%	$150	$750	($600)	(400%)
Total	100%	$15,000	$15,000	$0	

Imagine that your account has grown to $15,000. Those target allocation columns show you how $15,000 would be split among the asset classes using your chosen allocation. The actual column is what you would drop in based on what your fund balances actually are. The difference column shows you how far off your current allocation is from your target allocation. Fifty dollars on the bonds is no big deal, not worth making a trade just for that. The other ones are off, though. U.S. equities is 22 percent under-weight while international is over-weight (diet time!)

In this example, you don't have any commissions on buys. You would want to find out if there are any charges on sales, though. Again, if you hold ETFs for too short a time frame, you might be charged a fee, so check on any potential charges. If the fees are not an issue, then you could sell $1,450 of the international and buy into the U.S. and specialty funds.

If you have had some funds pay dividends, or make capital gains distributions, or you have accumulated cash through savings, do a quasi-rebalance with your new cash. Perhaps it is not advantageous to sell that international fund right away. Instead, you could use your $600 in cash to buy into the U.S. equity fund. As more cash builds up, you choose your next buy based on the asset class that requires more weight to get it closer to target.

Let's say that you have never added any money to this account, so the increase in value is simply investment returns (growth and dividends). This means that U.S. equities have had a bad run and international equities have had a good run. You sell out of international (at a high point) and buy in to U.S. equities (at a low point). *Emotionally, many people want to do the opposite.* If you do that, you would sell low (U.S. equities) and buy high (international). That goes against the "buy low, sell high" approach. A properly diversified portfolio always looks like some things are not working. When one asset class goes down, another goes up.

Using a rebalance approach takes some of the emotion out of the decision making.

Another consideration is that in a non-qualified account environment (individual account, joint account), your sales create tax consequences which you must consider, but not be completely driven by.

Tax Implications of Investing

The impact of investing on your taxes depends on your income level.

Dividends issued by a corporation (and passed to the investor through mutual funds) can be qualified or non-qualified.

- Qualified dividends are taxed at the capital gains rate (2014)
  - People in the 10 percent and 15 percent rate bracket pay 0 percent capital gains
  - People in the 25 percent, 28 percent, 33 percent, and 35 percent brackets pay 15 percent cap gains
  - People in the 39.5 percent bracket pay 20 percent cap gains
- Non-qualified dividends are taxed at ordinary income rates (regular tax brackets)

Capital gains (and cap gains distributions):

- Results from the sale of an investment at more than what you paid for it. A loss is when you sell it for less.
- Taxed at capital gains rates if the sale is long-term (you held the asset for more than one year before selling it).
- Taxed at ordinary income rates if it is short-term (original investment held for less than one year).

Capital Gain or Loss

Sales price − cost basis = gain (loss)

Mutual funds sell individual stocks all the time and create gains and losses. Usually at year-end, they pass these net gains along to investors in the form of capital gains distributions paid to the "shareholder of record" on a certain date.

Ordinary income rates: This rate is applied to your taxable income to determine the amount of taxes you owe. These are set by Congress and are based on your income level (a progressive tax system—you make more, you pay a higher rate) and your filing status (single, married filing jointly, etc.).

2014 Tax Rates & Tax Brackets

The IRS released the final 2014 tax brackets. Here are the federal 2014 tax tables:

Tax Rate	Single	Married Filing Joint	Married Filing Separate	Head of Household
10%	Up to $9,075	Up to $18,150	Up to $9,075	Up to $12,950
15%	$9,076 – $36,900	$18,151 – $73,800	$9,076 – $36,900	$12,951 – $49,400
25%	$36,901 – $89,350	$73,801 – $148,850	$36,901 – $74,425	$49,401 – $127,550
28%	$89,351 – $186,350	$148,851 – $226,850	$74,426 – $113,425	$127,551 – $206,600
33%	$186,351 – $405,100	$226,851 – $405,100	$113,426 – $202,550	$206,601 – $405,100
35%	$405,101 – $406,750	$405,101 – $457,600	$202,551 – $228,800	$405,101 – $432,200
39.6%	Over $406,750	Over $457,600	Over $228,800	Over $432,200

2014 Rates: If you are single and your taxable income (gross income – adjustments – deductions – exemptions) is $60,000, you are in the 25 percent bracket (the rate that applies to your next tax dollar). So here are your investment income rates:

- Ordinary dividends: 25 percent
- Qualified dividends: 15 percent
- Short-term capital gains: 25 percent
- Long-term capital gains: 15 percent

If you are married filing jointly and have taxable income of $60,000, you would be in the 15 percent bracket and ordinary dividends and short-term capital gains would be taxed at 15 percent. Qualified dividends and long-term capital gains would not be taxed at all (0 percent rate for people in the 10 percent and 15 percent brackets).

Regardless of what rates are in effect, if you have any of this investment income in a 401(k), IRA, Roth, or other qualified account, those accounts are not subject to any tax on the investment income. However, if you buy, sell, and receive dividends in non-qualified accounts, you will be taxed in the year of the transaction at the above rates.

You have no control over whether a stock or mutual fund pays out dividends or capital gains, whether the dividends will be qualified or ordinary, or if the gains will be long- or short-term. You do have control over whether you sell a mutual fund or stock. Ideally, you are investing for the long-term and have selected broad funds (like an index) so that you can hold and sell only to rebalance. If that is the case, be mindful of your acquisition dates so you know when a year has passed prior to selling if your investments are in a non-qualified account.

> **Tip:** Put funds that are known to pay dividends or make capital gains distributions in an IRA or other qualified account. For funds that are growth-oriented, keep those in your nonqualified account and try to hold for at least a year so that you have long-term gains.

When you complete your tax return, your short-term gains and losses will to be lumped together as will your long-term gains and losses. They can then be netted against each other to get either a net long-term or net short-term gain or loss.

Sell Methodology

For tax purposes, you must determine exactly which shares you are selling if you don't sell all of them at once. The way that you determine which shares you are selling is by using a sell methodology.

> **Note:** The following example is for educational purposes only, and should not be construed as investment advice. What is appropriate for you may not be appropriate for someone else, even at the same age, income level, or asset level, so you should always evaluate your own situation, objectives, and risk tolerance before making investment decisions.

Example:

	Shares	Price	Cost	Average
1/2/2012	100	$5.00	$500	
4/1/2012	100	$4.50	$450	
7/1/2012	100	$5.25	$525	
10/1/2012	100	$5.50	$550	
1/2/2013	100	$6.00	$600	
Total	500		$2,625	$5.25
3/1/2014	(250)	$6.25	Proceeds: $1,562.50	

The first five transactions are your purchase history. The 3/1/14 transaction is the sale. The broker is now responsible for tracking your cost basis, which is the details of how much each lot cost when you bought it. There are five lots of shares in the above example. Each lot had a different purchase price per share. The sell methodology choice answers the question, "Since you didn't sell all of the shares, which shares did you sell?"

You can use the following four choices offered by the IRS:

- **Average cost:** The $5.25/share is the average cost/share (total cost divided by the total number of shares). So your cost basis on the 250 shares was $1,312.50 giving you a long-term capital gain of $250.

- **FIFO:** First in, first out means what it sounds like: The 1/2/12 and 4/1/12 shares would be sold and half of the 7/1/12 shares would be sold. That gives you a cost basis of $1,212.5 and a gain of $350.

- **LIFO:** Last in, first out also means what it sounds like: The 1/2/13 and 10/1/12 lots would be sold, as well as half of the 7/1/12 lot. This gives you a cost basis of $1,412.50 and a gain of $150.

- **Specific identification:** You get to choose the lots that you sell. If you want to have a low capital gain, pick the most expensive lots to sell. In this case, that would be the same as LIFO. If you had a capital loss that you could use to offset the gain, you might want to have the biggest gain so you would sell the early lots (that works out to FIFO in this example, but it will not always, especially if your fund is volatile).

Average cost is the easiest way to go, as it lumps the shares together and the broker keeps calculating the average as shares come in and go out. There are rules about switching back and forth between methods, so it is best to pick one method and stick with it.

In years when you may have big capital gains, look for the investments that have losses and "harvest" the loss—sell the asset and wait at least 31 days before you buy it back (or buy back into another fund that isn't "substantially the same"). You lock in the loss for tax purposes.

You can also harvest the losses in a down year—$3,000 can be used to offset ordinary income and any excess can be carried forward. As long as you wait the 31 days before buying back the fund, you have a valid tax loss. If you buy back too soon or buy "substantially the same fund," the IRS calls this a wash sale and the sale is essentially voided for tax purposes.

Now you know about cost basis, sell methodologies, and dividend and capital gains rates. Here is the bottom line about investing and taxes:

- Understand the tax impact of your sell decisions, but don't make your decisions based solely on taxes.

- Try to put tax inefficient funds into qualified accounts. Research the fund's dividend history. If the fund is paying out a lot of current income, it is considered tax-inefficient. Tax efficient investments don't create a lot of current income. They may grow, but you have control over selling and creating a tax event.

- Try to hold assets in qualified accounts for at least one year to have long-term status.

- Try to match up gains and losses with the tax loss harvesting idea (consider short-term and trading fees to see if this makes sense).

If thinking about all of this paralyzes you, then invest in index-type funds that you plan to have for a long time. Rebalance by using new cash and dividend/capital gains distributions to buy in to the underweighted funds.

You will likely make some missteps; everyone does. Learn from each good and bad decision and keep investing. Most importantly, remove your emotions from the equation. Remember, sometimes when you climb a mountain, you have to walk through a little valley before you can reach the summit.

You can do it; just get started.

CHAPTER 9

Buying a House

In this chapter:

- The Language of Home Buying
- The Numbers of Home Buying
- How the Mortgage Market Works and Why You Should Care
- The Home Buying Process

Buying a house or condo is a goal for most people. The upside is that you are building equity (ownership) in an asset that has traditionally increased in value over time. Home ownership gives you more privacy than living in an apartment, and creates a greater sense of stability. On the downside, repairs and maintenance are your responsibility. No more calling the landlord to get things fixed. Other expenses range from purchasing a lawnmower to paying utility bills you never considered, such as water, trash collection, termite inspection, and pest control. There is no doubt that keeping a house up and running is expensive. It is critical that you know what you are getting into and make sure you can afford all of these costs.

This section is mostly about the logistics of buying a house. There is a multitude of information on this topic, so take to the internet if you want to learn more. The Department of Housing and Urban Development (HUD) website (www.hud.gov) has comprehensive information.

The Language of Home Buying

- **Mortgage:** This is the loan or "note" that describes the debt you are incurring and attaches the debt to the property you are purchasing. The mortgage is "secured" by the property via a "security deed" or "lien." This means that the company holding the mortgage loan gets the property if you don't make payments on the mortgage loan. The security deed is a legal document filed with the state that becomes public record.

- **Private mortgage insurance (PMI):** Insurance that a borrower may be required to buy if the down payment on the home is not high enough (usually 20 percent of the purchase price) to give the lender comfort that it won't lose money if the borrower defaults on the loan. It also may be required if the borrower has a low credit score.
  - Can be required to be paid up front as part of the closing costs or more commonly paid as part of the monthly mortgage and escrow payment
  - Rates are around $55/month/$100,000 of loan value

- **Down payment:** The amount of money you pay toward the purchase price in order for the lender to agree to loan the balance of the purchase price. A 20 percent down payment is required to get a conventional mortgage (also called a conforming loan). An FHA loan (one secured by the Federal Housing Authority) can be for 95 percent of the purchase price; however, the borrower must purchase PMI which is a form of insurance. VA loans (secured by the Veteran's Administration) have different lending requirements. The higher the down payment, the better the interest rate on the loan because the lender has less risk of loss even if the borrow defaults.

- **Closing costs:** These are all of the fees you pay to buy a house. These include: a loan origination fee, title insurance, property transfer fees, appraisal fees, and the list goes on. This is estimated at 3 to 4 percent of the purchase price. The lender will provide you with a good faith estimate (GFE) detailing these fees when you get the quote on the mortgage. The GFE tells you everything about the loan and the fees. The fees can change, but the GFE is usually pretty close to the final costs. Be aware that there can be snags which can cause fees to be higher.

- **Closing:** This is the process of signing all of the papers related to buying the house, securing the mortgage, getting the money to the right people, and finalizing the transaction. After closing, you own the home and are liable on the mortgage. You may go to a closing agent's office or the agent may meet you at your home to do all of the signing. More recently, people are using electronic signatures for closings and wiring the funds required to close.

  - **Closing attorney:** The lawyer who drafts all of the legal documents related to the transfer of property, the mortgage, and the securing of the lien on the property.

  - **Closing agent:** The person who takes the paperwork from the closing attorney and walks the buyer and the seller through all of the necessary signing. This may be someone who works for the closing attorney or it could be a paid third party.

  - **Closing statement (HUD I form):** This is the final accounting of all of the fees, who owes how much at closing, and who gets how much after closing. Structured similarly to the GFE in terms of the fees, the closing statement goes into detail about costs to pay off the existing first and second mortgages, how much the realtor gets in commission, how much the seller gets, and how much is paid to others in taxes and fees. It also details how much the buyer is paying for the down payment and closing costs, and how much and who is providing the mortgage loan.

- **Realtor or buyer's agent:** A realtor is someone who is licensed to sell real estate. Traditionally, realtors represent the seller in order to list[26] the house for sale on the market. With the rise of the internet and access to this system, the marketing side of buying and

---

26 List: Process of making a home available and known to realtors through the Multiple Listing Service (or System) (MLS).

selling a house is more accessible to people without a realtor; however, the legal logistics of buying and selling still require a realtor's expertise. A buyer's agent is a realtor who is helping someone buy a house, but not sell their existing house.

- **Escrow:** An escrow account is a type of account held by a third party (escrow company) for the benefit of someone else, and is to be used only as specified in the escrow agreement, typically to pay the property taxes and the property insurance on the house. In the house world, the company holding the escrow is the lender (or the loan servicing company). The person paying money into the account is the buyer of the house/borrower. If you, the buyer, are "escrowing" taxes and insurance, it means that these monthly costs are added to your monthly debt payment and then held in an account until the taxes and insurance are due. The escrow company (mortgage servicer or lender) then pays those bills on your behalf. PMI insurance, if required, is included in the escrow as well.

- **Foreclosure**: The process of taking the property due to non-payment of the mortgage.

The Numbers of Home Buying

- **20 percent** – down payment that you must make in order to avoid having to buy PMI.

- **31 percent** – the maximum mortgage debt-to-income ratio (total monthly mortgage payment divided by monthly gross income) that a lender will accept for a conforming loan. More conservative estimates say 28 percent.

- **36 percent** – the maximum debt-to-income ratio (total monthly debt payments—including daycare—divided by total monthly income) that a conventional lender will accept, although this may be lower in some cases.

- **41 percent** – the maximum debt-to-income ratio that FHA-insured lenders will accept.

- **80 percent** – percentage of home value that conventional mortgage lenders will finance. Hence, the requirement that the buyer make a 20 percent down payment.

- **95 percent** – percentage of home value that FHA-insured lenders will finance.

How the Mortgage Market Works and Why You Should Care

In order for a financial institution to provide mortgages, they need money. They get money from deposits (savings accounts or CDs). It takes a lot of deposits to get enough money to make one mortgage loan, plus the bank needs a reserve in case depositors want to withdraw money. In order to create liquidity to make more loans, banks sell their existing mortgage loans to investors. The big "investors" in this game are FNMA (Fannie Mae) and FHLMC (Freddie Mac).

Fannie and Freddie package the loans into groups and issue securities to other investors to get liquidity to go buy more mortgages. These securities are called mortgage-backed securities (MBSs). You could buy into a pool of MBSs if you wanted that type of investment, but often big institutional investors like pension plans and endowment funds invest in these. As the borrowers make payments on their loans, the repayments are passed through to the investors in the form of principal repayment and investment income.

In order for Fannie or Freddie to buy the loan, it must conform to their criteria in terms of amount (less than $417,000 in most areas of the country) and the borrower must have a credit score of at least 620 (as of this writing). Therefore, these "conforming" or "conventional" loans have the best interest rates since there is a ready market to sell them. You want to try to conform so that you can have the lowest possible interest rate (you saw above how much the rate matters.). Even though a 620 credit score conforms, it will carry a higher interest rate than a 720 credit score.

> **Loan-to-value (LTV):** The loan as a percentage of the value of the house. This is the inverse of the down payment. A 20 percent down payment equals an 80 percent LTV. Lenders talk about LTVs.

Some nonconformists can get loans too, though. The Federal Housing Administration (FHA) steps in and provides insurance (PMI) on loans that don't conform. So FHA criteria is less stringent than conforming loan criteria. These loans also have criteria, and the closing costs may be higher on an FHA loan. Of course, the borrower has to pay the PMI premium as part of the monthly payment. The VA (Veteran's Administration) has special loans just for veterans, so those loans have their own criteria.

The best scenario is to have a credit score in the excellent range (740+), provide a 20 percent down payment and get a loan for less than $417,000 so that it conforms. If you do that, you are well-positioned to get the best market rate of interest that you can get. As any of those things slip, the rate goes up. You also have to shop around. It is a competitive world out there, and different companies offer different rates and terms on the same day.

Mortgage Loan Terms

- **Interest rate:** Fixed rate versus variable rate.
- **Rate lock period:** The period of time that the lender will guarantee the interest rate from the date you lock it until the date the loan must close. A 30-day lock is a short time to get all of the closing stuff done. Typically, 60 days is more realistic.
- **Term:** 10-year, 15-year, 30-year.
- **Loan origination fee:** This is the fee charged by the lender to write the loan and is quoted as a percentage of the loan value. One to 2 percent is pretty common but you may get a no fee loan. Sounds awesome but look at that interest rate. The lender is getting their money somehow.

- **Points:** As you look at different rates, you will see that loans are quoted as "X percent at (zero, one, or two) points." What the heck is a "point?" Good question—a point is a percentage point, and it is based on the loan value so one point on an $80,000 loan is $800. Here is the deal with points. You pay the point as part of the closing costs to "buy down" the interest rate on the loan.

Example: Here is a real quote from 11/26/13 from the same lender (internet search): "4.625 percent at one point" and "4.875 percent at zero points." The $800 is buying the rate down 0.25 percent. A different lender gave a "4 percent at two points" and "4.125 percent at one point." The $800 is buying you 0.125 percent but you are starting with lower rates. You should ask: "what is the loan origination fee?" and "what is the lock period?"

The interest rate matters, especially over a long period of time, and paying cash up front will increase your closing costs.

The points decision has to be evaluated in terms of (1) whether you have the cash to pay the points up front and (2) the time period it would take to benefit from paying the point versus paying the increased interest. In other words, how long would it take you to "save" $800 in interest if you pay the lower rate on the loan?

- You can run an amortization table on the no points loan and then on the points loan and see when the accumulated interest on the points loan is $800 less than the accumulated interest on the no points loan. That tells you how long you would need to stay in that house and keep that loan in order to break-even on the points payment. Everything beyond that time will be interest savings.

- Here's a better idea: go to www.bankrate.com and search their calculators for the "which rate/points combination is right for you?" calculator, plug in your numbers, and shazam, it will tell you the break-even year.

- They also have a "loan comparison" calculator so you can input all of those different choices and figure out which one is best under different scenarios.

- Bankrate.com has about 27 different kinds of calculators for evaluating just fixed rate mortgages. They also let you compare today's mortgage rates using only your zip code. It also tells you what the P&I payment would be and how long the rate lock will last. It's a handy site although there are many, many sites that give you that info. I just trust this one.

- **Credit score needed:** The terms of the loan will vary depending on your credit score so when you look online, be sure you check to see what score is required to get that rate. Hint: they are going to display the 740+ rates first because those are the lowest rates. If you don't have above a 740, you need to click the drop down arrow and find your score.

  - On the same site, same day, same lenders, drop the score to 720 –739 and you'll get:

    - 5.125 percent at zero points and 4.875 percent at one point for the first lender. Basically, they are "charging" a point for the lower credit score.

    - 4.125 percent at one point and 4.125 percent at two points for the second. Hmmm, not sure who wants that two points deal . . . But they have 4.25 percent at zero points so they probably meant 4 percent at two points. So this lender isn't penalizing you for that 20 point drop in credit score.

  - Drop the score down to 660 – 680 and it is costing you an additional 0.375 percent, give or take. The site doesn't even quote below a 660.

  - Bottom line is that you need to work to get your credit score above 740.

The Home Buying Process

In a nutshell, here's what you'll go through:

1. Determine how much house you can afford.

2. "Practice" paying the higher mortgage as a way to save for the down payment.

3. Save the 20 percent down payment and the money for closing costs.

4. Get pre-qualified for the mortgage loan.

5. Determine where you want to live.

6. Look at houses.

7. Make the offer on the house you choose.

8. Go through the full underwriting process to get the mortgage loan.

9. Close on the house.

10. Move in!

1. Determine how much house you can afford

Rules of thumb for what you can afford:

- Approximately 2.5 times your annual income when you have other non-mortgage debt (car payments, credit card payments, student loans)

- Approximately four to five times your annual income if you do not have other debt

- **Ratios:** These are the maximum ratios that lenders usually require; however, you can be lower.
    - Keep the mortgage payment (including taxes, homeowner's insurance, and PMI) at no more than 28 percent of total monthly income (mortgage debt-to-income ratio).
    - Keep all debt payments at no more than 36 percent of monthly income (debt-to-income ratio).

Financial calculators: Go to www.bankrate.com for a free house buying calculator (there are many sites with these calculators) that allows you to enter your numbers and quickly see where you stand.

Example: You make $40,000 per year and plan to put down 20 percent of the purchase price as your down payment. Your monthly debts are:

- Car payment $250
- Credit card $100 (on an outstanding balance of $1,000)
- Student loans $300

Assume you can get a mortgage loan for 5 percent and you plan on getting a 30-year note.

The "times income" rule of thumb suggest that with income of $40,000 and non-mortgage debt, you are looking at about 2.5 times $40,000 which is $100,000.

A $100,000 purchase price means a $20,000 down payment plus about $3,000 to $4,000 in closing costs (estimated at 3 to 4 percent of purchase price), and an $80,000 mortgage loan.

Estimate that your homeowner's insurance will be about $500/year (this varies by area, so research costs in your city) and real estate taxes are about $1,000 per year. An average would be about 1 to 1.25 percent of the property value. This varies greatly depending on where you live, so plug in what is valid for your area.

- These will add about $125 to the monthly payment ($1,500/12)
- The principal and interest payment (P&I) on a 5 percent, 30-year, $80,000 loan is $430
- Total mortgage payment is $430 + $125 = $555

Review your ratios:

Mortgage debt-to-income: $430 + $125 = $555 divided by $3,333 of monthly gross income is 16.6 percent (versus a max of 28 percent).

You still technically have the capacity to borrow more based on this ratio.

Total debt-to-income: $555 + $250 + $100 + $300 = $1,205 divided by $3,333 is 36 percent (versus a maximum of 36 percent). Here, you have bumped up against the limit and should pay off some debt to make meeting your mortgage payment as well as other debt obligations easier.

A second way to approach this is to go online and search "how much house can I afford?" You will see many links to calculators that let you put in parameters much like what's outlined above. For example, per bankrate.com, you have capacity for a P&I payment of $430 which would equate to an $80,000 loan or a $100,000 house assuming a $20,000 down payment. So the 2.5 times income is pretty accurate in this situation.

The good news? There is no rush. Settle into your life, figure out your cash flow, and balance saving and debt pay-off. This is where you need to thoughtfully consider your priorities. How important are some of the "want to have" or "want to do" items in your spending, versus the goal of getting your own home? In other words, what are your "big rocks?"

Recommendations:

- If you are married, consider buying a home based on just one income even if both spouses are working. This sets you up for a much less stressful life. The extra income can be used for debt pay-off, saving for fun things, or improving the home. If one of you loses a job, gets sick, or is injured, the other income can help offset the lost income.

- Don't buy the biggest house you qualify for. Just because someone will lend you the money, doesn't mean it is good for you to take on that debt burden. And debt is a burden! Every month that mortgage company wants a payment. It is much more fun to have money to fix up a smaller house, furnish it, and decorate it than it is to barely make the payment on the bigger one.

- Determine what you can afford and then drop that number by 20 percent when you talk to the realtor. For example, if, based on your assessment, $100,000 is about the right purchase price for you, tell the realtor to show you houses with a maximum asking price of $80,000.

Realtors will try to creep up the price by showing you the beautiful house that is just a bit above your price. Remember, they get paid on commission, so it is in their interest to get you to purchase a home for as high as you can qualify for. That is not necessarily in your best interest, though.

Other Considerations:

- Housing is a lifestyle choice. It isn't a good investment, generally speaking, when you consider the costs of maintaining and insuring the home. Houses can and do appreciate in value, but as experienced in 2008/2009, they can also lose value.
- If you don't plan to live in the house for at least five to seven years, consider renting. You may not be able to build enough equity in the house to recover the costs of closing on the house, maintaining it, and insuring it.

2. "Practice" making the mortgage payment

Maybe you're living with your parents right now, so you have no rent, no utilities, and no grocery expenses. Ideally, you are paying big bucks on any debt you have (car or student loans) and are saving a truckload of money each month. You now need to get in the habit of "paying the mortgage," even though it is just to yourself.

Follow through on the example above. If the projected mortgage is $550, you need to write a check for $550 on the 1st of each month and deposit it to a savings account. You also need to determine how much utilities would be on a $100,000 house—gas, electric, water, internet, trash collection, exterminator, lawn maintenance, and homeowner's dues. This is tricky to get a feel for, especially heating and cooling, because it depends on where you live, how well the house is insulated, at what temperature you set the thermostat, etc. But you need to get a ballpark on it. Realtors are a great resource for this, or you can prowl around the internet and ask about costs in your area. Come up with an estimate and write that check too. Also, consider that you will have to buy groceries.

If you add all those things up, you are probably talking about $500 to $700 per month or more, on top of the mortgage, so the total amount you should put into savings would be about $1,000 to $1,200 per month. That puts you about 24 months away from having your down payment, and you will have that credit card paid off within a year or so. You will want to increase the savings (or debt repayment) by the amount you were paying. After doing that for several months, consider how the cash flow feels when you are putting that much in savings and paying your other bills. If it's tight, you may have to consider lowering the purchase price of the house or taking in a roommate to help cover expenses.

3. Save up the 20 percent down payment and the money for closing costs

This is all about prioritizing your goals and sacrificing small things for the bigger goal of owning the home. While you are saving, order a free credit report, correct any errors, document any reported issues, close unused accounts, and get your credit score up.

4. Get pre-qualified for the mortgage loan

Once you have the money in hand and are ready to start looking for houses, you want to get pre-qualified for the mortgage. Realtors like to work with pre-qualified buyers who have money behind them. Getting pre-qualified is the process of going through underwriting prior to picking out a house. Underwriting is the lender's process of checking out the quality of the borrower. Lenders want some assurance that you, the borrower, have the ability to repay the loan. During underwriting:

- You will fill out the loan application.

- The lender will ask you to provide:
  - Tax returns and W-2s (to prove the amount and consistency of your income)
  - Bank statements (to prove that you have the down payment and the closing costs)
  - Credit reports (which they will pull, but you have to authorize it)
  - Other financial details about your assets and liabilities

Who do you use for a lender?

- Look around the internet for mortgage rates. There are a lot of mortgage lenders, but be sure to pick someone reputable.
  - Do not put any personal information in the system at this point (other than zip code). Doing so might cause you to get inundated with emails and calls spewing information to every lender under the sun.
- Speak to your realtor. Realtors usually have loan originators they use and have worked with in the past.
- You could also ask your friends who own homes to offer their recommendations. Have your bank give you a quote and ask about their pre-qualification process.

Before you go to the lender, pull a free credit report again (see Chapter 5) and make sure all of the information is correct. The lender will verify everything you put on the application, so you have to bear your financial soul. By the way, fudging on a loan application is technically fraud.

Types of mortgage loans

Loans are categorized by rate (fixed or variable) and by term (10-, 15-, 30-year). Following is a description of various types of loans:

- Fixed rate loans have the same interest rate over the entire term of the loan. The most common mortgage for first-time homebuyers is a 30-year fixed-rate mortgage. A 15-year fixed-rate mortgage is a great option, but the payment will be much higher. When interest rates are low, you want a fixed rate loan because mortgage rates won't go much lower.

- Adjustable rate loans (ARM) have a much lower rate to start with, but will adjust at specified intervals to get to the market rate at the time of the adjustment.

There are limits on how much the rate can increase at each adjustment, but these are risky because you don't know where rates will be in 20 years. If you have an adjustment every five years, you can have five rate adjustments over a 30-year term. If rates were 15 percent, then maybe you take the bet that they will be lower in five years. However, you can always refinance the house if rates drop in the future.

Consider this: On your $80,000 loan, your payment is $430/month (P&I only) on a 5 percent loan. Increase that to 7 percent and your payment goes to $532/month. The total interest paid over the life of the loan is $74,605 versus $111,607. The rate matters and upward adjustments can crush your budget.

Before you pick an adjustable rate loan, read and understand all of the terms of the loan and carefully consider how long you expect to be in the house and where you think rates are going in the future.

5. Determine where you want to live

You probably have some idea about the location that you are interested in. Back in the old days, people drove around and looked for "For Sale" signs or scoured the newspaper for classified ads to figure out the housing prices in various areas. The internet is such a beautiful thing. Since you don't want to engage with the realtor in the "window shopping" phase, Zillow.com and similar sites provide a wealth of information and give you the luxury of window shopping right from your living room. Every realty company has a website with all of their listings.

Here are a few things to think about:

- Location is the most important factor in the price of real estate.

- Know the market where you are buying. Is it up and coming or slowly dying? What are the demographics: families with kids, retired people, singles?

- Schools are really important even if you don't have kids or plan to have them. People with children (potential buyers for your house in the future) care about good schools. A great school district will add value to your house.

- Think about access to amenities, grocery stores, restaurants, roads, highways, etc.

- How is traffic flow at rush hour?

- What kind of economic development is happening in the area that could increase or decrease house values in the near future?

- How active is the homeowner's association? You want to be around people who care about their community.

- Are the neighborhood and the common areas well maintained?

- Are there lots of homes for sale? Why?

- How old is the house? What has been replaced in the house?

- Search "things to consider before buying a house" on the web. You will get access to some good tips.

Typically, in order to actually see the inside of the house, you need a realtor. Some people sell houses "by owner" and they may have an open house on a weekend and allow potential buyers to stroll through. Realtors will often host these for their listings as well. Otherwise, your buyer's agent/realtor will make appointments to see the various houses in your area and within your price range. They typically have the key to a lock box which will get them into the house.

6. Look at houses

Before you look:

- Make a list of things that are important to you in a house, somewhat prioritized. Be clear about what is a "must have" versus a "nice to have."

- Use one copy of the list for each house you look at so you can check off the items at each visit. Take detailed notes and some pictures. When you look at multiple houses, they all start to run together so the better your notes, the easier it will be to compare houses.

- If you don't love it, don't buy it. Looking at houses gets old pretty quickly, but try to be patient and hang in there for the perfect house. The stronger the mental picture of that ideal house, the easier it will be to know it when you see it.

- As you start seeing some houses in your price range, refine your list of priorities and add or subtract your preferences based on the reality of your market. You won't get a 10-bedroom house with a pool for $100,000 unless there is something catastrophically wrong with it. (Can you say "nuclear waste dump?")

- Stay firm on your "magic number." It is easy to get caught up in the process and the desire to buy your own home, but remember that living tight is not very much fun. You will need money to decorate and furnish your house, not to mention to eat.

7. Make the offer on the house

After deciding on the house, you and the realtor will discuss how much to offer on the house. There is the listing price that the seller wants and there is what you are willing to offer. During the first week a house is on the market, it is unlikely that the seller will give much on the price. If the house has been listed for six months and the seller has already moved, there might be more room to negotiate. Realtors can help by knowing how much to offer. They understand the market and have a good sense of what is a fair price.

The realtor will submit the offer and if the seller accepts, you sign a contract specifying the terms of the purchase, and you pay "earnest money," which is a deposit toward the purchase. This shows that you are serious about buying the house and will result in the seller pulling the house from the market (or showing it as "under contract"). Having a realtor assist you with the contract helps ensure that you fully understand your obligation to purchase the house. You want to have some "out" clauses in case something is wrong with the house that you can't see, or if you change your mind.

You can also make the purchase contingent on something else, such as your other house selling. Sellers don't like contingencies, but that is part of the negotiation.

8. Go through the full underwriting process

The underwriting process includes:

- The lender finalizing their review of your creditworthiness: Even if you get pre-qualified, the lender will confirm that you still have your job, look at the bank statements to be sure you still have the money, and rerun your credit to be sure you haven't piled on a bunch of debt.

- You and the lender finalizing the details of the mortgage: Mortgage rates can and do change at least weekly so you want to watch the rates and understand how and when to lock yours in. The lock is only good for a certain period of time, so talk to the lender frequently and make sure the process is moving along.

- The lender finalizing their review of the property: This is their collateral after all. They want to be sure it actually has the value that the buyer and seller claim it has. This includes:
  - Ordering an appraisal, which is a report of the estimated value of the property performed by a licensed real estate appraiser.
  - Doing a title search (usually through a title insurance company). This involves a review of property records to make sure the property has no liens on it. Back taxes, contractor liens, homeowner association liens, and divorce settlement liens are some of the things that can impact the title.

- Ordering a survey of the property (an official drawing of the property, the boundaries, the houses, and any other structures on the property).

- Ordering a property inspection. This is a peek under the roof, so to speak, and is designed to find anything and everything wrong with the house. The property inspection also includes a termite inspection.

- The attorney drafting all of the legal documents to transfer the title, create the mortgage, and file the security deed.

Does all of that sound expensive? You're right, it is. Hence, the closing costs being 3 to 4 percent of the property value. Some of these fees may have to be paid up front, but most are part of the closing process. Your good faith estimate will outline all of this and your realtor will tell you what needs to be paid up front.

The reality of underwriting is that you do a lot of waiting and then there is some fire drill where you need to get some document or some inspection or some approval, and it is all of the utmost urgency and full of drama, and you race around and do everything and then . . . silence. Nothing seems to be happening until the next fire drill. It doesn't seem to matter how organized you are, there is always some kind of drama.

Here are suggestions to help curb the drama of the fire drills:

- Keep copies of everything you give them. This will be easy for you because you will probably load it electronically to a document portal.

- Keep a record of when you provide any documents, who you talked to, and the phone number or email address of the person. He who documents best, wins.

- Keep a log of every phone call, what they asked, and how you answered.

- Check in frequently and find out exactly what they are waiting on and when they expect to have it.

- Follow up. Create a reminder to touch base on the day the information is promised.

- Know exactly how long you have the interest rate locked in place and start raising the red flag if you are getting close to the expiration date.

Don't be surprised by anything that pops up. Know that it will work out eventually. Do what you can to stay on top of the process. The process is a pain, but a gazillion people make their way through it, so just dive in. Eventually, you get to the closing table.

9. Close on the house

The mortgage processor will one day call and give you the details of the closing, including where, when, and how much money you need to bring with you (or wire in advance). The traditional closing takes place at an attorney's office with you, the seller, and the attorney (or closing agent) sitting around a big table signing an enormous stack of papers. The attorney quickly talks you through what each paper means (you are assuming debt, the lender wants you to repay that debt plus a lot of interest, and if you don't, they can take your house). Please sign here and here and here and here if you agree to these terms.

You will either have pre-arranged a wire transfer to the closing attorney's escrow account, or you will show up with a certified check for the down payment and all of the closing costs. The good faith estimate form gets turned into the HUD1 form, which is the closing statement. This statement details all of those fees including who is paying them and who is receiving them. The bottom lines are:

- How much you must pay for the down payment and closing costs
- How much the mortgage company is lending you
- How much the seller receives, net for the house

Fortunately, although the underwriting processes can be maddeningly inefficient, most closing attorneys have their ducks in a row before anyone shows up at the table. You sign, hand over the money, and you get the keys to the house! You are now deeply in debt but remarkably happy, maybe even giddy, about it.

10. Move in!

This is the fun part! After all of that moving in and out of dorms or apartments throughout college, you finally get to plop down all of your worldly goods in your own house, where, hopefully, they will stay for a long time. Time to celebrate. You did it!

CHAPTER 10

~~Retirement~~ Financial Independence: You Gotta Save How Much?

In this chapter:

- Qualified Accounts: 401(k)s, IRAs, and Roths
- The Bottom Line

Chapter 4 covered the difference between retirement and financial independence. If you don't remember, here's a quick refresher.

Retirement	Financial Independence
Very far away, something that could never possibly happen to you.	Can happen anytime depending on circumstances.
For old people (you'll never be that old!).	For anyone who wants to be in control of their time without having to earn a paycheck.

The question you might be asking is, "How much money do I need to be financially independent?" You could probably fill a room with all the books, articles, and analyses that have tried to answer that question, but the short, quick answer is: it depends. (You knew that was coming, didn't you?)

Getting to the answer that's best for you takes estimating how much per year you will spend, and for how many years you will need that money. It all boils down to spending. How much of your accumulated assets will you burn every year in the pursuit of food, clothing, shelter, and lifestyle?

> **Rule of Thumb:** You can withdraw about 4 percent of your asset balance annually and it will theoretically never be depleted. Logic says that you have to earn at least 4 percent annually to make that happen. This is good for withdrawals today and going forward but maybe not so great for figuring out withdrawals 30 or 40 years from now. A little factor called inflation rears its ugly head. Remember that from Chapter 8?

If your assets are stored in your mattress, this rule won't work, but if they're in a diversified portfolio at a moderate level of risk, you should be able to sustain at least an average 4 percent return over long periods of time. With any average, there are highs and there are lows (market ups and market downs) but over time, your return averages out.

Example: You have saved $1 million. You can expect to withdraw $40,000 annually to cover your living expenses. If you need $120,000 per year to live on, you need $3 million saved, assuming no outside income during your financial independence.

In the financial planning world, sophisticated financial models are used to create probabilities of your assets lasting until age 90 or 100. To help you figure out if you can retire, how much is enough to retire on, and how much you can realistically spend in retirement, it is important to be more precise. For your just-starting-out purposes, 4 percent helps you frame it.

Having $1 million of savings might seem like a long shot when you are trying to pay off debt or buy a house and your savings are clunking along at a few hundred dollars per month, but money saved over time does add up. When you add the power of compounding, you start to get some nice balances, and 40 years of savings is a long time.

One way to get to your magic retirement number is to use qualified retirement accounts for your savings.

Qualified Accounts:
401(k)s, IRAs, and Roths

Any type of retirement account is "qualified" by the tax code, meaning that it has tax advantages with respect to the earnings and, possibly, the contributions. The tax code puts limits on how much money you can put in these accounts every year because, after all, the government isn't that generous.

401(k), IRA, other retirement accounts	Roth IRA
Contributions are excluded from income in the year you make the contribution. This is an adjustment from gross income to get to AGI for an IRA or an adjustment on your W-2 for employer plans.	Contributions have no impact on your taxable income in the year contributed.
Earnings are not included in taxable income in the year earned = tax-deferred growth.	Earnings are never taxed (assuming you meet the requirements) = tax-free growth.
Withdrawals are taxable income in the year withdrawn with no penalty if you are older than 59 ½.	Qualified withdrawals are never taxed.
10 percent penalty for withdrawing funds prior to age 59 ½, unless you meet one of the exceptions.	No penalty for withdrawal of contributions at any age; no penalty for withdrawal of earnings if the withdrawal is qualified.
IRS annual maximum contribution.	IRS annual maximum contribution.
Limit as to deductibility (IRAs) if income is too high or if you participate in an employer retirement plan. You can still make a contribution every year, even if it isn't deductible.	Limit as to ability to contribute if income is too high.
Required Minimum Distributions (RMDs) beginning at age 70½.	No RMD ever.
Employer plans may have an employer match (say dollar-for-dollar up to 3 percent of salary or something like that).	Some employer 401(k)s allow a Roth 401(k) contribution which follows the same rules as a Roth IRA except the contribution limits follow the 401(k) rules.

These accounts create a big tax savings. Whichever account you choose, you are deferring (and in the case of the Roth, avoiding) paying income tax on investment earnings, and in the case of non-Roth contributions, you are excluding the contribution from income. Over your lifetime, that can be huge.

- In the case of non-Roth accounts, contributions that you make are excluded from your current income. That means in the 25 percent tax bracket, a $5,000 contribution to a 401(k) or IRA will save you $1,250 in federal income taxes in the current year.

- Roth contributions do not save you anything on your current year taxes (no deduction for a contribution to a Roth). However, if you can contribute to a Roth, you will never pay any tax on the investment earnings over your lifetime (as long as you follow the Roth rules, of course).

> ### Roth Restrictions
>
> If you're single, making less than $114,000 (2014), you can contribute the full amount to a Roth. If you're married, filing joint, you must make less than $181,000 to be able to contribute the full $5,500/person.

- With non-Roth retirement accounts, you pay taxes on what you withdraw. The assumption is, though, that you will be in a lower tax bracket in your retirement years than in your prime earning years.

- 401(k) plans are employer-sponsored plans so if your employer doesn't have one, you are out of luck on that front, but they may have a Simple IRA or other plan.

- Even if your employer doesn't have a plan, you can always open an IRA. This is an individual retirement account, so it isn't linked to an employer except in the case of a Simple IRA which is an employer plan. Any financial institution (your bank) or online brokerage sites (TD Ameritrade, Schwab, Fidelity, e*Trade, etc.) will be able to open an IRA with a few clicks.

- The contribution to the IRA may or may not be deductible depending on your income level and whether you or your spouse participate in an employer plan. If you use any kind of tax software, it will calculate the amount deductible or you can go to irs.gov and search for IRA deductibility for all the details.

> The maximum IRA or Roth contribution in 2014 is $5,500 if you are under 50 years old. The 401(k) maximum is $17,500!

Make full use of these tax-deferred or tax-free accounts while you save for your financial independence. Every dollar of tax savings is another dollar toward your goals (rather than the government's).

The Bottom Line

The point of the whole financial independence discussion is that the amount needed in your retirement years seems big and completely out of reach, but it isn't. You can definitely get there. Here is what you do to move toward financial independence:

- Consistently save money starting today. If you can save 20 percent of your income, invested wisely, you will become financially independent. On a $40,000 income, that's $8,000 per year. At 5 percent return, that gets you to $1 million in 40 years, even if your income and savings never increased . . . but they will. Saving a lower percentage of your income will still get you to financial independence, it will just take longer. Regardless of how long it takes, time will pass, so start saving and build a plan to get to where you want to be.
- Be smart with windfalls. If you get a bonus or a gift of money, make sure you save some of it. It isn't all or nothing. How about 25 percent to savings, 25 percent to debt reduction, and 50 percent for fun or "stuff." It's tempting to go crazy with windfalls, but stay focused on your goals.
- Maximize use of qualified accounts (401(k)s, IRAs, or Roths) to save as many tax dollars as you can.

- Maximize free money. Employer match programs and other profit-sharing or stock purchase plans should be maximized. That money is on top of the percentage you save.

- Stay diversified when you invest. Sometimes in those employer plans, you are locked into the employer's stock. Diversify whenever you can and consider those holdings when you structure the rest of your investments (i.e., don't load up on U.S. equities in your other investment accounts).

- Live cheaply. Don't buy the new car; buy good used cars. Don't buy the absolute most expensive house you can qualify for; buy a house so that the mortgage is affordable now so you will have plenty for savings and debt reduction.

- Pass on the shiny object today in exchange for financial security. It is all about the big rocks. Don't be sidetracked by water and sand (all of the small trinkets); focus on your big rocks goals.

- Lose the "it's only five bucks" thinking. Remember, five bucks adds up. Apply this thinking when you are saving and paying down debt (I can add five bucks more to my monthly savings; I can add five bucks more to my debt payment). That adds up too . . . in a good way!

- Be consistent in monitoring your spending. Set your goals and adjust after mishaps. Just keep plugging.

- Use debt wisely!!

- Use debt wisely!!

Follow your passion and money will find you. When you chase money, it runs. Think of the guy chasing the next get rich quick scheme; it never happens. Money avoids him like the plague. Think of the quirky independents who are doing their own thing and being a genuine original. People are attracted to their unique passion, and will pay to get some of it.

As you consider how much you'll need to live comfortably into retirement, remember that even though goods and services cost more, income also goes up. More importantly, your investments get compounded (interest paid on interest) over time, which equals more money for you.

Follow the tips above and you will be well on your way to becoming financially independent; just make sure that as you make more, you save more. As you get 20 or 25 years down the path, you will see that the power of investing, maximizing employer plans, and consistently saving has served you well. At that point, you ratchet up the planning and look at some of the more sophisticated tools to create your path up the financial independence mountain.

Millions of people have reached financial independence. Getting there takes doing the work now, making the plan, and following through with it. You will never be sorry that you have money in the bank . . . never, but you may be very sorry that you don't. Money gives you choices. You may love your work and always choose to work, but maybe you love traveling or charity work or inventing quirky things or just hanging out. It would be nice to have the choice about how you spend your time. Money gives you that choice. Save now, make a plan, and you will have no regrets.

CHAPTER 11

The Legal Stuff: Who Needs What When?

In this chapter:

- The Last Will and Testament (Will)
- Powers of Attorney (POA)
- What Do You Need?

This chapter gets into some of the legal documents that are part of your financial life, or perhaps aren't, but should be. Don't worry, this will be fast and easy. By the time you need anything really complicated, you will be able to afford an attorney who will handle all of that for you.

By the way, nothing contained here should be considered legal advice, but it will give you some basic information. Note that state law trumps everything when it comes to legal documents. Every state is different, so always talk to an attorney before you do anything that has legal implications.

The Last Will and Testament (Will)

A will directs the executor (the person who carries out the terms of the will) to dispose of the testator's property after his death. The testator is the person drawing up the will, and he chooses a person to be the executor, usually a family member, but it doesn't have to be. After death, the testator is referred to as the descendant.

Your will tells the court who gets your assets when you die. It can also establish a trust or trusts, name guardians for minor children, and address items that impact federal estate taxes. Your will is a pretty powerful document. If you do not have a will and you die, the laws of your state of domicile (your legal residence) will determine how your property is disposed of. This is called dying intestate.[27] The rules around who inherits your property are the laws of intestate succession.

There are lots of documents to consider, but first, here's a summary of how assets transfer to others after you die.

- **Asset titling:** The way an asset is titled is the first determining factor in how that asset transfers to your heirs. There are several choices for most assets which require a title (house, car, bank account).

  - **Individual:** Assets with this title will transfer through your will.

  - **Joint tenants with right of survivorship (JTWRS):** As it sounds, the last man (or woman) standing (frequently a spouse) gets the account. The transfer to the other joint tenant is automatic once one of them dies.

  - **Tenants in common:** Two or more people share an undivided (or common) interest in the asset, with each having the right to possess the entire property. The interest can be equal or unequal, and upon death, the deceased's ownership of the property passes to his/her heirs based on the terms of his/her will.

  - **Tenants in the entirety:** This is similar to JTWRS, but it is reserved for married couples. It has the same result at death, the property transfers to the surviving spouse.

- **Beneficiary:** Retirement accounts will pass by beneficiary designation. These would be 401(k) accounts through an employer plan and the whole spectrum of IRAs, as well as pensions and any other

---

27 Intestate: Not having made a will before one dies or dying without a will.

account that is tax-deferred. Life insurance policy proceeds also pass by beneficiary. The account owner gets to choose a beneficiary or beneficiaries (see below for details on beneficiaries); however, if you are married and do not name your spouse as the primary beneficiary, your spouse must waive the right to the asset by signing the beneficiary form to indicate such. If your spouse chooses not to waive the right to the account, then the spouse will be named as the primary beneficiary.

- **Transfer on death account:** Some states allow you to assign a beneficiary to a non-retirement account (taxable account), such as your normal checking, savings, or brokerage account. Usually, you sign a separate form indicating the beneficiaries.

- **Will:** The final word on who gets your assets, if the first three situations do not make that determination, is your will.

Should you have a will?

The simple answer is yes, particularly if any of these situations apply to you:

- You have children (your will specifies who will be the guardians of your children after your death).

- You have financial responsibility for another family member (parent, sibling, etc.).

- You have a partner, but are not legally married (assuming you want your partner to inherit).

- You care who gets your stuff (or maybe more importantly, who doesn't get your stuff!).

- You want your assets to be used in a certain way after your death.

- You wish to leave money to charity.

- You have a high net worth.

- You want to make life easier for those left behind.

A will isn't the most critical legal document if you are single and have only the normal assets that a young, single person has. Most likely, if you died, your parents would inherit your assets. If it is important that someone other than your parents gets your assets, or if your parents are deceased, you may want to check your state intestate succession laws to determine what the succession rules are and then decide if it is worth a few hundred dollars to get a simple will drafted. You can Google "[state] intestate laws" and find links to specific code sections in your state. Nolo.com is a legal site that you could search to find this information as well.

If you are married with children, don't assume that all of your assets will automatically go to your spouse. Your children might end up getting a portion of your assets, which can make life a little more complicated for your surviving spouse. Asset titling (the legal title for your home, car, bank, and investment accounts) would be very important in this situation. If you legally titled these assets as joint tenants with right of survivorship then these assets would all transfer to your surviving spouse at your death, and having a will would not matter for these titled assets.

To help the rest of this chapter make sense, here is some vocab, because nothing says "fun" like a bunch of legal jargon!

- **State of domicile:** The state where you consider your home to be, where your mailing address is, where your driver's license is, and where you are registered to vote. You should have your will drafted in accordance with the laws of your state of domicile. This only gets tricky if you have multiple homes in multiple states.

- **Testator:** The person creating the will (you). The female is technically testatrix.

- **Executor/executrix or administrator:** The person you pick to be in charge of carrying out the terms of your will. Usually, this is your spouse if you are married, or it is a parent or sibling if you are single. Before you pick your party-hardy, unemployed brother to be your executor, think about the characteristics of a good executor. This should be someone who is:

  - Good about following rules

- Not intimidated by the legal process or attorneys, but has a healthy respect for them
- Responsible
- Very organized
- Dependable
- Able and willing to follow a task through to completion
- Sensible about business activities
- Willing to devote some time to the process

Think of your buttoned-up business types rather than your free-flowing artistic types. Administering a will can be an involved process (depending on the descendant's situation), can involve some paperwork, and definitely involves working with an attorney, so you want to think about a person who will be responsible and will take the process seriously. You also need to identify an alternate in case the first person is deceased or not willing to serve.

- **Guardian:** The person or people who will assume custody of your kids after you die. Usually, you will list your spouse first, but in the event you both die in a common accident or your spouse pre-deceases you, someone else needs to be willing to step in and care for your child/ren. This is not a decision you want to leave up to the courts or the outcome of a family battle.

- **Beneficiary:** A person who will inherit something in your will, get the benefit of a retirement account, or receive the proceeds of a life insurance policy.
  - **Primary beneficiary:** This person/people will definitely inherit if s/he/they are living and there is something to inherit.
  - **Contingent beneficiary:** This person/people only inherit if all of the primary beneficiaries are deceased and there is no per stirpes clause (or it is irrelevant because none of them have lineal descendants).

- **Per stirpes:** This is language that helps to determine what will happen to a beneficiary's share if s/he is deceased. A per stirpes designation means that the person's child/ren (or other lineal descendants) will step in to the place of the deceased beneficiary. Per stirpes means "by branch" so think of the family tree. The money stays "on the branch" of the deceased's beneficiary.

- **Per capita:** This is another possible designation to determine what will happen to a beneficiary's share if s/he is deceased. Per capita is "per person," so the remaining beneficiaries would share the deceased's part of the inheritance without regard for other lineal descendants.

- **Trust:** A trust is a legal entity, administered by a trustee, which can own assets. Such assets must be administered in accordance with the terms of the trust document. The trust document will name the beneficiaries as well as how, when, and under what conditions the beneficiaries will receive both the income from the trust and the "corpus" (assets owned by the trust). Trusts can get very complicated, and there are many types and uses for trusts. They are commonly used to protect assets or to specify exactly what the assets may be used for.

  - **Testamentary trust:** A trust created by a will. It is irrevocable once created because the creator of the trust has died so the terms cannot be altered. It is only created once the testator has died and the estate is being administered.

  - **Intervivos trust (living trust):** A trust created while the grantor (creator of the trust) is still alive. These can be revocable or irrevocable depending on the terms of the trust (the wishes of the grantor).

- **Probate:** The legal process of proving that the will is valid and of administering the estate.

Most people don't think about death, certainly not a 20-something year-old, but it happens to everyone. The bottom line is that having a will lets you communicate your final wishes, and it makes it easier on the family and friends you leave behind. If you die intestate, the court has to appoint an administrator for your estate. Your family will have to petition the court to ask to be appointed. If there is conflict among the family, this process can create issues, especially when several people think they should be appointed. On the other hand, if you don't have a lot of assets, there isn't much to fight about.

A word about online, do-it-yourself wills: Yes, you can buy software or forms online and create a will yourself. But be very careful. Legal terms can be confusing and the will must comply with state laws, so sometimes having a poorly drafted will is worse than having no will at all.

Powers of Attorney (POA)

A POA lets you give your legal power to someone else who will stand in for you if you are unable to represent yourself. That someone is known as your "attorney-in-fact" or your "agent."

Types of POAs

- **General:** A general POA allows your indicated agent to act on your behalf in a variety of different situations.

- **Durable:** General, financial, or health care POAs are made durable by adding language that makes the POA remain in effect or take effect if you become incompetent or incapacitated. The point of having a POA is so that someone can take over if you become unable to manage your own affairs or make decisions on your behalf.

- **Financial:** A financial POA allows someone to conduct your financial business for you. This can be broad, such that the agent can do just about anything you can do. This is commonly used by a person in the military who is deployed. She might give her spouse a general POA so he can handle her financial affairs while she is deployed (pay bills, sign tax returns, etc.).

- The financial POA can also be "special" meaning that the POA is limited to one transaction or one type of transaction or is for a limited, defined period of time. This would be used if you were going out of the country for three months and needed someone to pay your bills for you, although with online banking, this is becoming less of a need than in the past. Another example is that you may need someone to sign the papers when you buy a house, but you are out of town the day of the closing. The POA would be limited to just this one, specific transaction.

Imagine how traumatic it would be for your family if you were involved in a horrible accident and were injured to the point that you could not make decisions or speak for yourself. Yes, your family could petition the court to have someone appointed to take care of your financial affairs, and it would all work out, probably. Sounds like a hassle, right? You bet it is . . . attorneys, legal proceedings . . . is that what you think your family wants to be doing if you are in the hospital? What if your family is not the type that you would like to have banging around in your bank account? What if you are living with someone (not married) and now your significant other and your parents are fighting about who takes the financial reins? This can get ugly quickly. Durable financial POA saves the day. You have already identified who takes the reins. Done deal.

If you Google "durable power of attorney" there are lots of sites that will sell you a form. It would probably be OK to use a form, but make absolutely, positively sure that you understand everything.

- **Health care:** A health care POA allows you to appoint someone (typically called a personal representative) who will make health care decisions for you if you become incapacitated. It only goes into effect in specific, predefined situations when you cannot make decisions for yourself. There are two types of health care directives:

    1. **Living will:** A living will allows you to express your wishes in the event you become incapacitated. In the living will you are able to tell doctors or a hospital what you want or don't want in terms of life-sustaining procedures.

    2. **Advanced Health Care Directive (Advanced Directive):** Some states have created this form in order to combine the health care POA and the living will into one document. In some states the document is fairly detailed and allows you to go down

a list of situations and make specific choices about what you want to have happen to you in these situations. These documents only come into effect if you are mentally incompetent, brain injured, comatose, or terminally ill.

Google "Terry Schiavo" and read through all of the results. Yikes, that was a tragic situation. It was a major ordeal for her, for her family, for America, for the courts, and it went on for years! Regardless of who you think was right—her husband for wanting to suspend life-support or her parents for wanting to keep her alive at all costs—the tragic thing is that Terry didn't get to tell anyone what she wanted. Enter the health care directives.

- A health care POA would have let Terry pick someone (her husband, her parent, some objective third party) to make these decisions for her. Yes, it would be tough to be the agent who has to decide. So . . .
- A living will would have let Terry make those decisions for herself, in advance. She could have checked the box "I want life-support" or "I do not want life-support." Then everybody would have known.

The site www.caringinfo.org has links to the health care directives for your state. Download it now and start thinking about what you would want. Look at the form for your state and see if you feel comfortable completing it on your own. If you don't, the website has people you can speak with, or you can consult with an attorney. Hopefully, you will never need that form, but fill it out anyway and get it executed (legal speak for getting all the right signatures in place). You will likely need witnesses and/or a notary to make it legally enforceable.

The Caring Info site also has good information on what to do with your document once you sign it. Obviously, it can't be used if no one in your family knows you prepared it.

The Terry Schiavo case received a lot of media attention. It was a shocking example of the importance of planning (or not) one's final wishes and directives in the event of incapacitation. Don't think "the speeding truck" would never happen to you. It happens every day to someone.

What Do You Need?

You definitely want to have a durable financial POA and some kind of advanced health care directive once you reach the age of majority in your state (18 to 21 years old). These are important because (1) they make life so much easier for your family in the event that something really bad happens to you, and (2) they allow you to decide, in advance, how you want your affairs managed in your absence, death, or disability.

CHAPTER 12

Money: The More You Have the Better You Like It!

In this chapter:

- Energy To Money Formula
- The Secret To More Money
- The Turbo-Charger
- What's the Main Thing?

Money is energy, plain and simple. Humans had to create something tangible to represent their energy in order to make it easier to exchange.

Think about the cavemen days when there was no money or gold or anything at all to use as a medium of exchange. The cavemen bartered; one guy wanted something that the other guy had so either he clubbed him over the head and took it, or he started offering up things he owned which could be traded. Maybe somebody had meat and somebody else had berries. The two had to haggle to figure out how many berries would be equal to how much meat. At the very core of that exchange was the fact that one guy exerted effort to kill an animal to get the meat and the other guy exerted effort to pick all of those berries. There are other factors that enhance or detract from how much value is placed on that energy. Things like scarcity, access, and difficulty of obtaining will make the meat or the berries more or less attractive. Since each caveman was different, there was a different value placed on every exchange.

Fast forward a few hundred years, and the energy that was traded was more likely to be physical energy: the energy used to grow vegetables versus the energy used to milk cows. People traded sacks of flour for eggs or milk or a visit to the doctor. The doctor gave not only the energy of examining you but the stored energy of years of studying medicine.

So this isn't some new-age "think about money and it will show up" philosophy. This is about turning your physical or mental labor into a paycheck. By working, you literally turn your energy—mental or physical—into money. The energy you give exactly equals the money that you earn, assuming, of course, that neither party is taking advantage of the other.

> Volunteering works the same way as your paid labor, only you don't get paid in money; you get paid with other energy, but that's a different conversation.

Energy To Money Formula

At the most basic level, this should tell you that if you want to have more money, you need to give more energy. Sounds logical. If you work more hours, you'll make more money. However, the reality is that some energy commands more money than other energy. The trash collector working for an hour gives an hour of energy just like a brain surgeon gives an hour to an operation, but the two will not walk away with the same amount of money.

The key to having a lot more money is to:

- Invest more energy;
- Invest that energy to fill a need; and
- Invest that energy consistently for the amount of time required.

If the need you fill is in high demand, then many people will want the energy you have, and they will be willing to pay for it. So much the better if no one else has the ability you have.

You don't have to become a brain surgeon to have energy that is in demand; you can refocus your energy right now in your current job and make yourself more valuable. The energy to money formula is:

invest energy + fill a need + consistency + patience = more money

Consider your current job. Your boss has a need in his role at your company. Find out what he needs, see how you can fill that need, and you have just made yourself more valuable to him. You have directed your energy toward filling his needs. Even by doing your normal job with more focus, more creativity, and more dedication, you are expending more energy and therefore, eventually, the money will follow because energy must be in equilibrium. If energy gets pushed out from you, it changes the flow and creates space in you that will need to be filled with more energy. It's just like when you breathe out, your lungs must refill with air to fill in the space left behind. Same thing with money, but the process has to start with you giving the energy. You can't breathe in more air when your lungs are full nor can you take in more energy if you haven't expended it first.

In times of economic hardship, when jobs are hard to find, a creative person will find a way to fill a need. She will give the energy first and know that she will ultimately be rewarded for the effort, for the energy she invested.

If you could see the life of very successful people before they were successful, you would see that they invested enormous amounts of energy before finding success. Thomas Edison tested thousands of materials for the light bulb before he found the one that worked. Thousands! That is a lot of energy invested before the energy of success came back to him. Michael Jordan shot a lot of basketballs before signing with the Bulls. Tiger Woods invested thousands of hours on a golf course before anyone knew who he was. The brain surgeon spent thousands of hours investing his mental energy into learning before he got the first dollar of repayment. The energy equation always works when it is given the time to work. The doctor can't quit after the first year of med school; he hasn't invested enough energy or enough time to complete the cycle.

Anybody can wake up and become a garbage collector. That job requires a one-hour energy commitment to complete the cycle and earn the hour of wages. But that hour of wages earned has to be less than the hour earned by the surgeon because the surgeon's energy investment was really the thousands of hours of med school, internship, and residency that occurred prior to performing the one hour of surgery.

This has nothing to do with the importance of the job. Ask anyone who hasn't had their trash picked up in a few weeks during a hot summer. That trash collector is really important to them, more important than a brain surgeon because they don't have an injury that requires brain surgery. This concept goes back to filling the need. The advantage that the trash collector has is that everybody needs their trash picked up every week. This is a very high need in society. The disadvantage is that the only energy required to perform that job is to get up in the morning and get to it; low total investment of energy equals low-paying job. It's still a really important job, though, so the job isn't low paying because society doesn't value it; it's low paying because the total energy investment required to do it is low.

The Secret To More Money: Consistency and Persistence

Perhaps you are an entry-level employee at a corporation. You and all of the other entry-level workers have invested about the same level of energy in your degree or training, so you start off with roughly the same pay, and you are expected to do the same job. If you expend more energy in your job either by working faster, increasing your knowledge of the company or the industry, or by using creative energy to think of ways to accomplish your objectives more quickly, more efficiently, or with fewer errors, you will create an imbalance in the energy equation. Imbalances cannot stay that way for long. Eventually, if you consistently give more energy, you will receive more money.

It could be that at raise time, the boss has a range that he can use, say 0 to 5 percent. Or he may have $X that he has to divide among the employees in his group. Because you already invested the energy, you will get a bigger piece of that pie than will the guy next to you who just showed up and gave the minimum energy to keep his job. Or it may be that your boss's boss sees your results being consistently above your co-workers and understands that you are ready for a bigger challenge, so you get promoted. Or it may be that the manager in the department next to yours sees that you are working beyond the energy required for your job and pegs you as a go-getter. The next time a position opens in her group, she may approach you, and you will be able to command a higher rate for your hour of work because you already invested the energy.

One more thing to clarify: You must invest that energy to fill that need on a consistent basis for the amount of time required. Con-sis-tent. That means you can't be a go-getter one day and a slacker the next. People won't trust you, and they won't know what to expect. No one in a position of authority wants to risk getting the slacker on a day they need the go-getter. They will stick with what they know and what is reliable, dependable, and consistent.

Dictionary.com defines persist as "to continue steadfastly or firmly in some state, purpose, course of action, or the like, especially in spite of opposition, remonstrance, etc." To "persist" involves being consistent, being dependable, and sticking with it even when you don't feel like it, when you're tired, cranky, and just plain sick of it. Persistence is a pretty important quality.

If you want more money, then:

invest energy + fill a need + consistently + persist + be patient = more money

Speaking of being a go-getter, read the book, *The Go-Getter* by Peter B. Kyne. It's a tiny book that'll take you less than an hour to read, but it sums up the whole money equation in one little story. Go-getters get rich (assuming they don't blow all their money on stupid stuff).

The Turbo-Charger

There is one more element that will make the money equation work a whole lot faster, with a whole lot less effort on your part, and that is passion. If you are investing energy in something that you absolutely love doing—something you are excited about, something you jump out of bed to do, something you would do all day, every day, even if you weren't getting paid—the energy you invest won't feel like working. It won't feel like you are depleting yourself; it won't feel like the life is being sucked out of you when you invest that energy. That is exactly the way you know for sure if you are doing the right thing with your life or the wrong thing.

When you do what you love, you are fueled by your passion, not by your muscles or your brain. You tap into a source of energy that you can feel moving through every fiber of your being. Time seems to stop. You don't get hungry or thirsty or tired. You just ride the wave of this energy, this excitement, this passion. When that happens, when you are in the zone, magic happens. Then your investment of energy doesn't feel like an investment out of you, a taking away, a giving up of something; it feels like energy in, a getting, a receiving of something. Wow, how great is that?

The magical part of that cycle is that not only does it not feel like working or struggling or forcing, but others feel that energy of passion, and they are attracted to it. They feel that you are riding the wave and not fighting the current, and they want to be closer to that energy. The people who need the energy that you have will be pulled like a magnet to you and to what you are doing. This might not happen instantaneously, but it will happen. Once you start putting that energy out, it creates the vacuum for you to pull something in—more energy, more money. When you keep doing the things you love doing, when you quit chasing money and instead chase passion, the energy of money will eventually find you.

The reality is that you have to eat in the meantime. You have to pay back your student loans and pay rent and utilities and buy clothes. You might have to pick up some trash to pay for all of that while you chase your passion after hours. You might not enjoy it at first, but you realize that it's a really important job and someone has to do it. Then you begin to see that job as one of the most important jobs in the world. You see the huge benefit that you give to society by picking up that trash. You view your role from 8 to 5 as to be the best darn trash picker-upper the world has ever seen. You find a reason to be passionate about picking up trash for those eight hours a day. Then, suddenly, the days go by faster; it doesn't seem like work so much as a calling. You can still access the energy of passion instead of the energy of depletion once you change the way you view the work you do right now.

So, the ideal thing is to pursue your absolute passion and get paid for it today. If you aren't getting a paycheck for doing what you're passionate about, keep pursuing your passion. Keep doing what you love in your spare time—even if you're not getting paid to do it—and stay open to the ways that you can turn your passion into an income-generating career. Follow your passion, and envision yourself spending your days in this environment of energy and money flow. When you stay open to the possibilities, eventually your dream of making a living through your passion will become a reality. It may take time. You may experience what seem to be setbacks, but in reality those are opportunities to expand yourself. Don't feed into the energy of frustration or impatience, because that absolutely cuts you off from the flow of energy you need to ride to your dreams.

Energy Zappers = Money Zappers

Frustration and impatience come from forcing. Whenever you start to feel the emotions of frustration and impatience, remember this: trust, grow, let go. Trust that this is all part of the process of becoming. Grow into who you need to be to take the next step. Let go of everything: your plan, your time frame, your expectations, and your preconceived notion of how things are supposed to be.

Believe that everything is exactly as it's supposed to be, happening exactly as it's supposed to happen to get you to be exactly who you are supposed to be. Consider that everything prior to this point—the pain, anguish, missed chances, blown opportunities, mean people, bad parents, horrible Christmases, ruined vacations, and bad jobs—were actually supposed to happen. When you accept your past and expect great things for your future, your energy for the present increases.

Some people who ended up being thankful for the "bad":

- Viktor Frankl
- Nelson Mandela
- Ghandi
- The Dali Lama
- Abraham Lincoln

That's pretty good company to keep.

What's the Main Thing?

The main thing isn't about making money, it's about the adventure of life. It's about pursuing your passion, helping people, getting the help you need, doing what you were put on this earth to do, giving the gifts that only you can give, and being supported and sustained while you do what you love to do.

Lots of people get it screwed up and think that they have to have money to do the things they love to do. But that's backwards. You get money when you do the things you love to do. And when you get the money, you usually find that it doesn't really matter because money is just a blip on a piece of paper that the bank sends you. What you really want, what you really need, is to express your true self, to give your gifts to the world, and to be seen and valued for who you are. Money gives you none of that.

Money doesn't help you become who you are meant to be. It doesn't help you give your gifts to the world. It doesn't force you to invest your energy and find your passion and overcome your obstacles. Society inundates people with messages that money is the goal. In reality, money is simply a sign that society values your gifts and your energy.

It all comes down to: Why do you want money?

Read the parable of the fisherman to help answer this question:

> A boat docked in a tiny Mexican village. An American tourist complimented the Mexican fisherman on the quality of his fish and asked how long it took him to catch them. "Not very long," answered the Mexican.
>
> "But then, why didn't you stay out longer and catch more?" asked the American.
>
> The Mexican explained that his small catch was sufficient to meet his needs and those of his family.
>
> The American asked, "But what do you do with the rest of your time?"
>
> "I sleep late, fish a little, play with my children, and take a siesta with my wife. In the evenings, I go into the village to see my friends, have a few drinks, play the guitar, and sing a few songs. I have a full life."
>
> The American interrupted, "I have an MBA from Harvard and I can help you! You should start by fishing longer every day. You can then sell the extra fish you catch. With the extra revenue, you can buy a bigger boat. "
>
> "And after that?" asked the Mexican.

"With the extra money the larger boat will bring, you can buy a second one and a third one and so on until you have an entire fleet of trawlers. Instead of selling your fish to a middle man, you can then negotiate directly with the processing plants and maybe even open your own plant. You can then leave this little village and move to Mexico City, Los Angeles, or even New York City! From there you can direct your huge new enterprise," the American explained.

"How long would that take?"asked the Mexican.

"Twenty, perhaps 25 years," replied the American.

"And after that?" the Mexican asked.

"Afterwards? That's when it gets really interesting," answered the American, laughing. "When your business gets really big, you can start selling stocks and make millions!"

"Millions? Really? And after that?"

"After that you'll be able to retire, live in a tiny village near the coast, sleep late, play with your children, catch a few fish, take a siesta with your wife, and spend your evenings drinking and enjoying your friends."

Surely you can see who is the wiser of the two. Generations past bought into the MBA philosophy of chasing money, needing bigger, and more, more, more so that someday, they could relax and enjoy it all. Maybe that was not the best approach. You are at a stage of your life where you can step back from this paradigm and choose what is most important to you, decide how much is enough to meet your needs, and allow yourself to live the life you want to live. The fisherman was actually living the dream without having a lot of money in the bank or sacrificing 25 years of 18-hour work days to make it happen.

Stop right here and ask yourself:

- "What am I working for?"

- "Why do I want money?"
- "What is really 'the dream?'"
- "Can I have 'the dream' even without having a lot of money?"
- "What is the most important use of the money I earn?"

Those answers should direct your actions going forward. The answers will change over time, but you should plan to re-evaluate the questions periodically, especially if you have a significant other. It is important to be sure you are both on the same page with your answers to these important questions.

You can get more money. You have the money equation, and you can give the energy for as long as it takes. Just be sure you want to. Be sure that the energy you give is used in pursuing your passions and sharing your gifts rather than chasing money. Choose wisely; that will make all the difference in whether you have a lot of money and are happy or you have a lot of money and are miserable.

CHAPTER 13

Money Mistakes

In this chapter:

- Common Money Mistakes
- Emotional Spending
- Know What You Are Really Trying To Buy

Millions of people make mistakes with their money in many different ways, yet few are willing to admit it. What better way to help you make smart decisions with your money than by learning from how others screw up with theirs? So here's where I become transparent to help you avoid some common money mistakes. I have made many money mistakes throughout my life, and I've witnessed others do so too.

Without further ado, here are my top money mistakes and some ideas on how to avoid them.

Common Money Mistakes

- **Didn't track my spending:** I started out making pretty good money, but I would get to the end of the month and there was nothing left. I could never fully pay off my credit card. I didn't have a lot of stuff, but the money seemed to evaporate, for years! I could always pay my bills, but I didn't know where all that money went.

Remedy: If you don't know where your money is going, you certainly can't change your money reality. You must understand your money metrics, set goals around money milestones, and monitor changes over time.

- Use some kind of system for tracking where every dollar goes. Software is available, mint.com is a useful cloud-based solution, an Excel spreadsheet or template works, or a plain old pad of paper and pencil will get the job done.

- At my firm, we help clients look at their cash flow in terms of five areas:

  1. Taxes

  2. Charitable giving

  3. Savings

  4. Debt servicing

  5. Lifestyle costs

These are the only places that money goes. The first four categories are pretty straightforward, but here are some thoughts:

  1. **Taxes:** Taxes are the toll for living in the greatest country in the world. If you don't like how the government is spending your money, get involved. Otherwise, accept that this is the price of playing, be honest on your tax return, and enjoy freedom.

  2. **Charitable giving:** Consider how important it is for you to support causes that you believe in whether they are religion-based, people-based, or results-based. Allocate the amount or percentage that feels right for you.

  3. **Savings:** Obviously, you want to get that savings number as high as you can; 10 to 15 percent will change your life if you save it consistently.

  4. **Debt servicing:** Focus your efforts here until you have no debt except your mortgage, then create a plan to get

your mortgage paid off. Being free from debt is the first step to being financially independent.

5. **Lifestyle costs:** The lifestyle number should be further broken down so you can see, at a minimum, what you are spending in fixed costs, variable costs, and discretionary expenses.

□ **Fixed:** You are locked in to paying $X/month for something (rent or an insurance premium).

□ **Variable:** You have to pay it every month, but it varies month-to-month. These are utilities, food, etc.

□ **Discretionary:** You didn't have to buy it, but chose to. This is all the fun stuff, the eating out, the accumulation of goods. No one wants to live like Scrooge, but if you become more thoughtful and selective about your activities and your accumulation of shiny objects, you will be more financially secure, and you'll never miss those trinkets that seem important in the moment. Like most people, you probably have way more than you need. Besides that, the excitement of something new fades quickly.

- **Didn't have any money goals:** When I was young and single, I was just winging it, doing pretty much what I wanted and basically not paying much attention to anything but the next paycheck. I learned that I had to point myself in some direction or I would drift along ending up who knows where. Think about what is important to you (remember those big rocks?)

Remedy: Consider the following questions and set some goals.

- How much emergency savings will make you feel safe? When would you like to have that amount? How will you make that happen?

- When will you be debt-free? Do you have a strategic plan to make that happen?

- How are you creating wealth? How much money do you want working for you through investments? What is your monthly goal for increasing your wealth?
- How do you want to allocate your fun money? Is it stuff or experiences? Is travel or more education a priority for you? Starting a business? Buying a house?
- Pick your big rocks and create a plan to make them happen.

- **Carried credit card debt:** When I first started working, I always seemed to have a balance on a credit card. I never looked at the cost of carrying that debt. Paying for yesterday's pleasure stinks, though, and the true cost of whatever sale item was purchased three months prior was far above the actual full retail price if I finance it with a credit card. The high cost of credit cards was explained in Chapter 5. Just say no.

  Remedy:

  - If you have a balance on a credit card, make a plan to get it paid off, pronto.
  - Stop charging things to credit cards unless you specifically set aside the money to pay the bill in full at the end of the month.
  - Keep credit cards at home if you are an impulse shopper.
  - Stay away from online shopping if this is your weakness. You can put stuff in your cart all day long, just don't check out.

- **Didn't have an emergency savings:** I didn't build up a real rainy day fund when I first started out. I had some cash in savings, but not to the level that I should have.

  Remedy:

  - Accumulate at least three months of expenses in cash (six months is even better). Life happens. It will rain on your parade at some point. If you have cash socked away, life's emergencies aren't such a big deal, and you aren't forced to use expensive credit card debt to save the day.

- **Not comparison shopping, sale shopping, or couponing:** My 23-year-old self was a full retail shopper. I didn't love shopping, so I would go to the store only when I needed something right then. I didn't plan ahead. Need a dress for a wedding? Run to Macy's two days in advance. Want a new car? Drop by the dealership after work. I had no time for bargain hunting. I was a working woman, busy, busy, busy! This was not a good approach.

  Obviously, when spending money, it makes sense to spend the least amount possible to get what you are buying. For me, this is a time versus money issue. I don't like going to three or four places to compare and bargain shop. There is a cost to that in terms of time and gas.

  Remedy:

  - Be mindful of comparison shopping, but also be smart about it. Remember, time is money.

  - As extreme couponers make headlines, couponing has become very popular, so there is definitely value there. Perhaps dip your toe in by looking at the Sunday paper, clipping some coupons, or using the grocery store sales flyer to plan your meals for the week. There are also lots of websites to help you take advantage of coupons. The savings is worth it when you make a commitment to couponing.

  - For big-ticket items, definitely figure out when the stores have sales and how you can time your purchases to take advantage of sales.

- **Did not have an investment strategy for my 401(k):** I started out putting money into my 401(k) as a 23-year-old (what a wise gal I was!). I didn't want to lose any money, so I invested it in the guaranteed interest fund . . . whoops. All of those prime growth years, and I was basically going backwards because that interest was not even close to keeping pace with inflation, let alone doing any high-powered growth.

Remedy:

- Understand your investing time frame and create an investment strategy that maximizes your growth over that time frame.
- Review the fund choices, do some research on what is appropriate, and be sure to rebalance annually or semi-annually.
- Understand that the market goes up and it goes down in the short-term (weeks, months, years). Over decades, it goes up.

- **Had an "it's only five bucks" mentality with respect to spending, but not with respect to saving:** My cart at Target was always over $100. Going in for toothpaste? I have to walk past the book section, ooh, there's the CDs, and now back to the makeup aisle. It was so easy to toss things into the cart without considering the cost.

  This was covered earlier. But every dollar matters, and every dollar going out the door takes away from your wealth while every dollar in the bank adds to it.

  Remedy:

  - Stop the constant drain of cash out. You don't need to be a cheapskate, but throwing money to the wind won't bring you happiness either.
  - Spend wisely and with purpose. Five bucks matters. Period. Strike "it's only" from your vocabulary.

- **Panicked and sold investments at the bottom:** This is really two mistakes rolled into one. I didn't have enough emergency cash, so when the market went off a cliff, I sold because I couldn't afford to lose any more. If I had had myself positioned correctly with my emergency fund in cash or CDs, I could have tolerated a drop in the market. I could have waited out the rebound and never taken a loss.

  Remedy:

  - Have your emergency fund in cash and CDs so you don't have to worry about market fluctuations eating away your peace of mind.

- Avoid panic when the stock market does what it does. "Be fearful when others are greedy, and greedy when others are fearful." That has worked pretty well for Warren Buffett . . . you know, if you like taking money advice from a billionaire.

There are a lot of money mistakes you could make throughout your lifetime, and most of them can be avoided by paying attention, spending with purpose, and having a plan. If you use your money purposefully, you will be fine. More importantly, when you make a money mistake, recognize it, learn the lesson, and refocus. Mistakes happen in every area of life. You grow and learn the most from your own mistakes, so consider these money mistakes as tuition paid. There is no final exam, though, as the class never ends, so it's best to learn the lesson the first time.

Emotional Spending

Some people tend more toward emotional eating than emotional spending, but it's the same basic thing. You are down for whatever reason and to get a little pop of good brain chemicals, you run to the mall or sit down with a catalog or jump on your computer and buy some new, shiny objects. Perhaps instead—whether you're an emotional spender or an emotional eater—you should grab your running shoes and pound the pavement for 30 minutes. Your brain, your body, and your net worth would be much better off!

What's really happening?

There are lots of psychological studies that explain that the human brain has a very sophisticated system for regulating moods and for recognizing and reacting to pain and pleasure. There is an enormous physical and mental bias in most people away from pain and toward pleasure. Eating, like shopping, creates a feeling of pleasure, causing happy brain chemicals to be pumped out, and the bad mood is gone . . . temporarily.

The other thing that happens is that shopping (or eating) distracts you. It takes your attention away from the unfairness of your boss and puts it on a new outfit, shoes, or cool gadgets. The problem, other than too much stuff and massive credit card debt, is that you don't actually address the issue that has you feeling bad. So tomorrow, back at work with the unfair boss, you will feel bad again. You have that bias away from pain (feeling bad about anything ever) so back to the mall you go. This creates a pattern, so that after a fight with the boyfriend—shopping! After a disappointment—shopping! After looking at your credit card statement—shopping! This isn't working well.

Ideally, when you feel bad, you need to reach for a notebook (rather than a catalog or cookie) and hash out how you feel, why you feel that way, and how you can create a plan for resolving the situation. The solution is to feel what you feel and resist the urge to medicate with shiny objects (or cookies, or booze, or whatever). No magic bullet; feel it and deal with it. The sense of power and accomplishment should give you all the good brain chemicals you need. This takes both self-awareness and a commitment to do the hard thing that you don't want to do—have the conversation with your boss, find a new job, or talk to HR. None of that is fun, none of that will make you feel good immediately, but you have to be willing to feel bad for a while as you work through resolution of the problem.

Common Forms of Emotional Spending

Heat of the moment spending: This is when the emotion and the stuff get meshed together. The remedy is to realize it in advance and plan for it. Recognize what costly and unnecessary items or experiences get you excited (or depressed) and ready to whip out your credit card. Is it electronics, clothing, jewelry, weekend getaways, tattoos, sporting events, concerts, household items, gifts for others, or something else? Is it the job, your spouse, your parents or siblings, the economy, the weather, your friends, your body image, or something else that tugs at your emotions enough to push you toward spending? The remedy with any of the emotion-based issues is to first recognize that you are susceptible to these emotional triggers and then make a plan in advance to deal with it. Prepare to win; don't have your credit card with you!

Immediate gratification: "I want an Oompa Loompa NOW!" Do you remember the horrible little girl from the Willie Wonka movie? Oh, she was awful, and she lives in every one of us. I want, I want, I want. You want what you want when you want it. TV has convinced you that you deserve to have it, too, and right now. Finance it today! Take it home now! Oh, those advertisers know how to reach in and talk to that bratty little kid inside of you.

You can't let the bratty little kid run the show, though. That kid will have you in the debt ditch faster than you can say Oompa Loompa! The only remedy here is to keep that Oompa Loompa girl in mind and laugh when you hear yourself say, "I want." Recognize and (gently) acknowledge your internal brat, then be the adult and ignore it.

You want in the immediate moment, but then it's usually gone quickly if you just wait it out, think about what you want most (the big rocks), and move on. If there is something that keeps reappearing, then maybe it is time to move that to big rock status and make a plan to get it. There is nothing wrong with wanting to have nice things, but getting those things in a purposeful way in alignment with your most important values is the sign that you have moved from Oompa Loompa girl to powerful adult.

If I only had _____ then _____ syndrome: "If/then" thinking can be another spending trap. "If I only had a new laptop, then I could write my book." "If I only had a bigger house, then I wouldn't fight with my husband so much." This thinking pattern is part excuse (the lack of a laptop is the problem, not sitting down and doing the work of writing) and part rationalization to give Oompa Loompa girl what she wants.

The remedy to this kind of thinking is to reverse the sentence, "How can I write my book even though I don't have a laptop?" "How can I stop fighting with my husband even though I don't have a bigger house?" The issue is that Oompa Loompa girl isn't really that interested in writing a book, she just wants a new laptop and is working an angle to get one. You have to call her on her baloney and see reality as it is: plenty of people have written great books without a laptop.

What's her name wrote her book on her Blackberry! The thought probably makes your thumbs ache just thinking about it, but if there is a will, there is a way.

Call a spade a spade and cut to the real issue. A goal can be achieved in many ways. Buying a shiny object is probably not critical to the process. Stop with the excuses, rationalizing, and distractions and make a plan to solve the problem, achieve the goal, or get to the finish line in a way that is aligned with your spending priorities.

But it's on sale: It will be again! You are still spending money even if you are paying 50 percent less today than you would have yesterday. Focus on the big rocks. If this is a big-rock item, then definitely wait until it goes on sale and save some money. If it is not a big rock, think of how much money you are spending. Spending. What else might you do with that money? Pay more on your debt? Add to your travel fund? Weigh that sale item against your big rocks. There is always something else you could be doing with that money.

Avoidance: Many people are conflict-avoidant. They will do almost anything to avoid confrontation, disputes, and hurting others' feelings. This often takes the form of spending on non-big-rock items, often in the form of buying gifts to ease the pain of themselves or others. This is not a good thing for obvious reasons. Adults speak openly and honestly with each other to resolve problems. Money conversations should be no different.

If you fall into this category, you have to start anticipating where these situations will arise and have a plan going in. Maybe you have to decide that you will be uncomfortable at the table when your friends are deciding how much each owes on the dinner bill. Perhaps you need to create a plan to address your friend who owes you money. Maybe you need to gather your roommates and lay out the facts about the bill sharing and create an agreement if you are being left holding the bill bag. Whatever money issue you are avoiding must be acknowledged and addressed. This is not fun, but it is a growth opportunity. Don't expect it to be easy. It's OK; you can do hard things.

Filling the hole: There is a time in everybody's life where they feel an emptiness or loneliness. Maybe all of your friends have a significant other and you are unattached. Maybe you are new to the city or the company and don't have a social circle yet. Maybe you have ended a relationship, finished school, or lost a loved one. Wanting to fill the void is a natural reaction, and filling it with stuff is very common.

If you are facing an empty spot in your life for whatever reason, identify it and find ways to fill that void with happiness and satisfaction that lasts longer than the item you bought. There is always someone lonelier than you, so find a cause that is important to you and fill that space with volunteering. Take a class or work on a project. Just as with the other areas of emotional spending, recognizing the pattern is half the battle. Creating a plan to address the real issue is always the best solution.

Know What You Are Really Trying To Buy

Power suits (so '80s), sports cars, the latest and greatest iToy—these are prime status objects that marketers love to bait you with. Why do you take the bait? You're trying to buy something that can't be bought, but, oh, how you want to believe it can be. The old guy buying the sports car might be trying to buy his hotness back. The up-and-coming executive is trying to buy acceptance and a spot at the table with the expensive suits and leather briefcase. Millions of people try to buy "fit and thin" every January with an assortment of videos, weights, gadgets, and diet books.

Stop and think about what you're really trying buy. There is no magic in the shiny object; it cannot give you confidence that you don't already possess, and it can't earn you a promotion that you don't deserve. Some things simply are not for sale. The sooner you recognize that and get to the heart of the matter, the sooner you can take the action that will get you what you really want.

And so on . . .

The list of reasons you spend money goes on and on, and is as individual as each person. Recognize your triggers for spending emotionally/irrationally/not based on your priorities. Be aware of your emotions, first and foremost, and then develop a strategy for handling those situations. Waiting is always a good one. Delay spending as long as you can, but make saving something you do today.

What Is Your Financial Plan?

In this chapter:

What Is A Financial Plan?

A financial plan is how you intend to use your money. If you received $1,000 right now, you would probably begin mentally creating a $1,000 financial plan. You would know how to allocate it to things that are important to you. So, in a nutshell, that's a financial plan. There is nothing particularly mysterious about creating a written financial plan. Simply:

- Assess what your financial life actually is like. Gather facts about your current situation. Write down your balance sheet and cash flow so you know where you are starting and can use it to measure your progress.

- Define what you want your financial life to be like. Do a lot of soul-searching about what you want out of life, how your money can best serve you, and how it can help you create the life you want.

- Write down goals, tweak them, or change them.

- Develop action steps that move you from where you are to where you want to be with specific dates when those actions will be completed.

- Implement the plan by taking the results you imagined on the paper and making them real in your everyday life.

- Evaluate the plan, your actions (or inactions), and fix what isn't working.

- Make mistakes and missteps and learn from them, then get back to what is most important.

- Repeat the process again, and again, and again.

Financial planning is a simple concept, but it takes time, persistence, and dedication to go through the process. And it is a process. This isn't something you do and check off the list. It is an iterative process. Most people have pieces of their plan in their heads: paying the bills, buying a house, paying off debt, etc. But in terms of a detailed, written plan, few people have one.

Financial planning involves a lot of small but important steps. To make it easier to digest, this chapter is divided into sections:

- Section 1: Your Financial Plan

- Section 2: Long-Term Goals

- Section 3: Protecting Yourself and Your Family

Before you dive in, make the commitment to set aside at least 30 minutes to work on the first section.

You will need:

- Either a notebook, pencil, and a calculator, or a blank Excel worksheet
- Your last month's spending details (checking activity and credit card or other loan activity) or access to your Quicken or mint.com account

Feel free to copy the worksheets in this book so you can use them each month, or you can easily recreate them in Excel or download the template from the website, www.graduatesguidetomoney.com.

The starting point is to evaluate objectively what your financial life is like right now. Consider these categories:

- Balance Sheet or Net Worth
  - Investments
  - Property
  - Debt
- Cash Flow
  - Paying the Bills
  - Charitable Giving
  - Savings

> Your balance sheet is created as of a point in time because the balances change day to day as you make money, spend money, pay debts, etc.
>
> Your cash flow covers a period of time because it is the cash received or used over a specific period of time (usually a month, quarter, or year).

Grab your pencil (or your mouse) and get to work!

SECTION I: Your Financial Plan

Balance Sheet or Net Worth

Your net worth is simply what assets you would have left if you paid all of your debts. It is also called a balance sheet because in accounting lingo, you want the accounting equation Assets = Liabilities + Owner's Equity (net worth) to balance. This equation is simply Assets − Liabilities = Net worth (equity) reordered. The easiest time to create a balance sheet, in the old, pre-online days, was to get your statements at the end of each month and tally up the values of all of the bank accounts, as well as the credit cards, and find your net worth. Today, you can do it right this minute by logging in to those websites or pulling up your Quicken or mint.com accounts.

Why do you care about your balance sheet? Plain and simple, it is a measure of your financial security. It doesn't matter if your goal is to be a millionaire or if you don't care a bit about being rich, being financially secure is important for everybody. Even if you don't care about wealth for the sake of wealth or if material things are not important to you, you still want to be able to take care of yourself in good times and in bad and to be able to support your family. Understanding your net worth helps you frame your financial security.

Consider these two situations:

- Mary, age 50 and single, has a net worth of $200,000 (meaning that she could pay off all of her debts and still have $200,000 available to her).
- Jill, age 50 and single, has a net worth of $1,000.

Both of them make $40,000 per year and need a minimum of $2,000 per month to pay for rent, utilities, food, and other expenses. Both have the same health insurance, but neither has any disability insurance. They both have a heart attack on the same day and neither one can work for three months while recovering.

226 | The Graduate's Guide™ to Money

Mary can manage without working for 100 months given her net worth. Jill, not so much. Jill is in big trouble the first month. That is an example of financial security. You may think you would never have a heart attack or get sick or get into an accident or lose your job, but it happens every day to someone. Your net worth is your cushion when you fall or get knocked down.

So, take a look at your balance sheet right now:

Balance Sheet as of _____:

Assets		Liabilities	
Cash (checking)	_____	Bills that are outstanding	_____
Emergency cash fund	_____	Credit cards	_____
Long-term savings	_____	Student loans	_____
IRA/401(k) accounts	_____		
Car	_____	Car loan	_____
House	_____	Mortgage	_____
Other assets	_____	Other debt	_____
Total Assets	_____	Total Liabilities	_____
		Net worth (assets − liabilities)	_____

If your liabilities exceed your assets, you are technically insolvent; however, if you are young and have a high student loan balance, that will skew the information. The student loans are the investment you made to increase your future earning power. That earning power is an enormous asset that can't be put on the balance sheet.

One thing to notice on the worksheet is that your liabilities are matched with the asset that they closely relate to. For example, you will use your cash to pay bills that are outstanding. So your emergency fund up is matched up with your credit cards just to see if you have enough in savings to get rid of the credit cards. That gives you a sense of how things line up and whether you are lop-sided or out of balance. Ideally, you want to have more total assets than total liabilities. That's the picture of where you are.

Now, take a look at where you want to be. The table allows you to project your ideal balances in the next three months. This provides a short-term, realistic, achievable goal for you to work toward, rather than something as long-term as five years from now.

Ideal Balances

	As of	In three months	Change
Assets			
Cash cushion* (checking)	_____	_____	_____
Emergency cash fund	_____	_____	_____
Long-term savings	_____	_____	_____
IRA/401(k) accounts	_____	_____	_____
Liabilities			
Credit cards	_____	_____	_____
Student loans	_____	_____	_____
Car loan	_____	_____	_____
Mortgage	_____	_____	_____
Other debt	_____	_____	_____

*"Cash cushion" is in your checking to represent what you usually have left over at the end of the month. You should set a goal for what that

cushion should be. This is that little extra that helps you feel secure in knowing that if something small happens, you can cover it. Aim for a couple hundred bucks, at least.

For now, fill in these three columns: where you are today, where you would like to be in three months, and the difference. Before you get to six-month and nine-month goals, take a look at your monthly cash flow so you have a sense if the plan can work. Cash is king!

Flip back to Chapter 3 and review the spending plan. If you use Quicken or mint.com, go to last month's actual numbers. If you completed the simple cash flow plan in this book, (inputting all payments by date from 1st to 31st), get that out now and take a look at last month's actual numbers. If you don't have any of that, take the time now to complete the simple cash flow plan from Chapter 3. You need these numbers to move forward with your plan.

Now that you have that in front of you, here are a few questions:

1. **Solvency:** Do you consistently have enough money to pay all of your bills (at least minimum payment) every month? If yes, go to step 2. If not, continue through the bullet points below:

- Create a detailed budget that shows how much money you have coming in each pay period and what bills have to be paid.

- Look at each bill that is paid and analyze how you could reduce or eliminate that expense.

- Create a detailed list of action steps to implement these ideas and include what you need to do (call the cable company to eliminate the premium channels), what items you need (write down the phone number, company hours of operation, account number), and when you plan to do it (Tuesday during lunch hour).

- Update your detailed spending plan to reflect the new, lower amount of that bill.

- Consider carefully what you can sacrifice in the short-term to reach your financial goals.

- Implement your plan and monitor it for a couple of months to make sure it is working. Keep refining it until you reach the point that living this way is automatic. Then go to step 2.

2. **Debt reduction:** Are you able to pay off the balances of all of your credit cards each month? If yes, go to step 3. If not, continue through the same six bullet points above:

- If you have credit cards with balances, go through the debt reduction approach in Chapter 5. Until you have your credit card debt paid down and are able to pay off the balances each month, it is hard to progress toward other goals.

- Make a plan and implement your plan. Perfection isn't possible, so cut yourself some slack and get back on track after slip-ups.

3. **Charitable giving**: Do you believe in the concept of tithing or giving something to organizations that support your religious or philanthropic views? If this is not important to you, go to step 4. Otherwise:

- Determine a percentage of your income you are willing to contribute and can comfortably give to support these causes. Calculate the amount of your giving and add that line item into your monthly spending plan.

- If a percentage isn't important, figure out the dollar amount you want to give and add it to your monthly spending plan.

- You may want to integrate a charitable giving plan before you tackle paying your credit cards in full each month. That's fine. Do what you feel is best for you.

4. **Analyze your spending:** At this point, you have the basics covered. You can comfortably pay all of your bills each month, including your credit card balances in full, and you have incorporated your charitable giving intentions into your spending plan. Now, complete this pictorial of your cash flow.

Start from the bottom and work up. Write in the actual amounts in the lower boxes and then total them up and write the total in the upper spending boxes. Of course, your monthly income is whatever it is.

When you complete this chart, you'll see the big picture of your spending.

Actual Uses of Cash

Now that you've done this exercise, you know where your money is going. Here is the gut check on it: how do you feel about where your money is going? How do you feel about your giving number? How do you feel about your savings number? Are some of those boxes empty? Are there more boxes that you want to add? How do you feel about your debt reduction number? Would you like to see fewer boxes in that area? How do you feel about your lifestyle expenses? Specifically, look at the categories below it. Is enough money or too much money going toward the "nice to haves" and "entertainment" boxes?

Write down what you want this chart to look like given your current income:

Ideal Uses of Cash

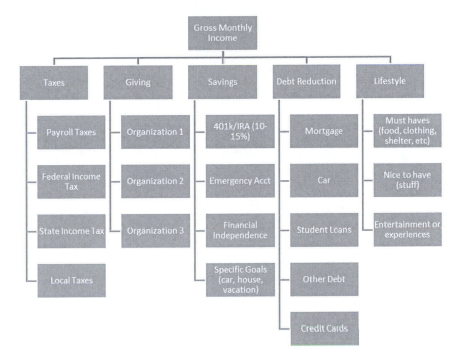

Now, write down your priorities, in order of importance, for the steps you can take to get your chart from where you are to your ideal chart above. For example, if you currently spend more money on "stuff" than you feel good about, and you would like to shift that to paying down credit cards, you would write: 1. Reduce my "stuff" spending by $50/month and increase my payment on my ABC credit card by $50/month beginning mm/yyyy.

Complete your priorities list now:

1. _____

2. _____

3. _____

4. _____

5. _____

6. _____

7. _____

8. _____

9. _____

10. _____

11. _____

12. _____

13. _____

14. _____

15. _____

16. _____

17. _____

18. _____

19. _____

20. _____

Take a breath. This is hard work, and you have done well to get this far. Look at your priorities listed above. Is there anything that seems out of order? Make sure that these items that are important enough to you that you will take action on them.

With these facts in front of you, go back to the first section with the balance sheet goals. Take a look at those original goals you set for three months from now and answer these questions:

- How do those balance sheet goals for adding to assets or reducing debts line up with my spending realignment priorities?

- Are they in sync?
- Given my priorities above, is it realistic to achieve those balance sheet goals?
- Are there conflicts?

Think through your answers and then go to the next exercise where you will expand on the balance sheet goal section. You will merge your "wishful thinking" numbers from the Ideal Balances table and the "cold hard facts" from the cash flow exercise. In the following table, put in your number as of today. In the "In three months" column, record your new goal that takes into account the priorities you wrote down.

For example, for your cash cushion (checking), perhaps you would like to always have at least $500 of cushion in case you make a math mistake or something weird comes up. Perhaps as of today, you have a cushion of about $100. What will you do over the course of the next three months to move toward the goal of having $500 of cushion? Maybe you take out $60 each week in cash for whatever. You are willing to drop that to $40 per week to move toward this goal. $20 per week times about 12 weeks is $240. So in the chart below for cash cushion, you would say $100 for "As of today" and $340 for "In three months," and in the last column put "reduce cash withdrawal to $40/week." For this to work, you need to be more thoughtful before whipping out your cash over the next three months. You don't want to trade a cash buy for a credit card buy. You have to stick to only spending $40 each week on your miscellaneous purchases.

This is where you move from hoping and wishing that things will change, to actually creating a realistic strategy to make it happen. You have to identify a specific action that will purposefully and strategically get you the balance you plan for.

Go through this exercise of dropping in your numbers for each line item and projecting what those balances will look like in three months given the spending priorities you listed. Be sure you indicate specifically how you will move that balance. What are you willing to give up in order to move your balance sheet in the direction you want?

3-Month Spending Plan

	As of today	In three months	Change	How are you going to achieve this?
Cash cushion (checking)				
Emergency cash fund				
Long-term savings				
IRA/401(k) accounts				
Total assets				
Liabilities				
Bills that are outstanding				
Credit cards				
Student loans				
Car loan				
Mortgage				
Other debt				

Great job! Now, project another three months out. Put your "In three months" numbers from the chart above into the following chart and project for the next three months. Think about the example above on the "cash cushion." As previously stated, in three months, you should be at $340 of cushion. You only need another $160 to hit the goal. That means eight more weeks of allowing that extra $20 per week to build up. What will you do with that $20 per week for the remaining four weeks? Will you go back to your $60 per week spending or will you apply that to another of your spending priorities?

6-Month Spending Plan

	In three months	In six months	Change	How are you going to achieve this?
Cash cushion (checking)				
Emergency cash fund				
Long-term savings				
IRA/401(k) accounts				
Total assets				
Liabilities				
Bills that are outstanding				
Credit cards				
Student loans				
Car loan				
Mortgage				
Other debt				

Excellent! The next two sections will allow you to project a year from today. If you put pen to paper (or curser to Excel spreadsheet), you can see that these projected small changes in your spending can result in big changes in your balance sheet fairly quickly. The cash cushion goal was achieved within five months just by cutting back on cash spending by $20 per week. Then, if that $20 per week is put toward goal 2, you will achieve goal 2 quickly. By rolling the money from goals 1 and 2 toward goal 3, your results will really start to progress.

9-Month Spending Plan

	In six months	In nine months	Change	How are you going to achieve this?
Cash cushion (checking)				
Emergency cash fund				
Long-term savings				
IRA/401(k) accounts				
Total assets				
Liabilities				
Bills that are outstanding				
Credit cards				
Student loans				
Car loan				
Mortgage				
Other debt				

Now, one more to get your projection out to one year from today:

12-Month Spending Plan

	In nine months	In twelve months	Change	How are you going to achieve this?
Cash cushion (checking)				
Emergency cash fund				
Long-term savings				
IRA/401(k) accounts				
Total assets				
Liabilities				
Bills that are outstanding				
Credit cards				
Student loans				
Car loan				
Mortgage				
Other debt				

Fantastic! You did a projection that is based on real actions, so you now know exactly what you have to do and for exactly how long in order to hit the mark. The good news is that you created a financial plan. The bad news is that now you have to execute the plan. It has to come off of this piece of paper or off of your computer screen and into your daily life to become real. DAILY. Day one when you step up to the ATM, you have to type in 4-0.0-0 instead of 6-0.0-0, and each day as you pull out your wallet to buy something, you have to consider whether what you're buying is worth it, given that you have $20 less in your wallet. And, sometimes, maybe many times, you will have to say "no" to that thing in order to make your three months goals a reality. You have to stay home when the gang wants to go out. You have to walk away from the department store sale. You have to go to the library instead of Amazon.com. You have to make your lunch instead of going to the deli at the office. You have to make different choices than you made last month, otherwise your numbers won't change. It's that simple and that hard.

You need a mental plan as well as a financial plan because logic doesn't work very well when you can smell that coffee or see those shoes or feel the pull of your friends wanting to go out. You must make a mental plan in the warm exhilaration of the financial plan that you just crafted. Make the plan while you're buzzing from the picture of your ideal spending plan and the promise of your balance sheet three months, six months, a year from now. Think about how much your assets could go up and your debt could go down. How many of your goals can you achieve in that short time?

Identify the challenges that you will face in executing on your plan, and what you can do or put in place to overcome those obstacles.

Challenging situation	When it occurs	Plan for overcoming it

Consider getting some buddies to join in the financial fun and help each other stay accountable. Also, just so you know, you aren't perfect. All the great planning and advance considerations of the challenges won't get you there 100 percent of the time. Some days you are tired and grumpy and you just want a $5 cup of coffee, dang it! No worries. Small steps applied consistently will take you around the world if you keep stepping.

Recap:

1. You checked in on your financial situation, your balance sheet, as of right now.

2. You set some goals on what you would like your balance sheet to look like in three months.

3. You went through your cash flow (spending plan) looking at what you spent last month.

4. You categorized that spending into the five spending buckets: taxes, giving, savings, debt reduction, and lifestyle. Hopefully, you broke down the lifestyle piece into "must haves," "nice to have," and "entertainment or experiences."

5. You reviewed that spending in light of how it made you feel. This is the personal, emotional part that sometimes gets lost in the numbers. These feelings may tie into your money story, so think through that.

6. You created your Ideal Spending Plan based on your current income.

7. Next came the priorities for what changes to your spending were the most important to you. This is when you moved from what you actually spent to what you would ideally spend.

8. Armed with this information, you revisited the balance sheet to see how the three-month goals looked in light of your information about your ideal spending plan. The goals were reworked, if necessary, and you also wrote down specifically how you would be able to accomplish each of the goals within three months.

9.   You then projected out to the six month, nine month, and one year anniversaries using this same strategy.

10. The next step was to create the mental plan to think through the obstacles and challenges that you may face along the road to new and goal-focused spending habits.

11. Now, put those action steps and that mental plan someplace where you can review it daily. This has to become top of mind, and the only way to do that is to make sure it is in front of you regularly. Book an appointment in your calendar to review these goals and priorities and then evaluate how you did at the end of the day.

12. Now, go out there into the world and make it happen. Day by day, decision by decision, you must choose to go in the direction of your plan or to wander and see where you end up. Choose wisely.

Moving Forward: Accountability, Progress, Rewards

This isn't the end of the line on the spending topic or the goal setting process. You made all these plans and you executed on the strategies to move you from the balance sheet you had toward the balance sheet you want. At the end of the first month (or more often), you have to check in, see how you did, identify which goals you hit, which ones made some progress, and which ones still need your focus.

Look at the specific action steps you created in your plan:

- Rate yourself on a scale of zero to three with zero being "I did zero" and three being "I nailed it!"

- What's your max possible score given your goals? How did you do? You can totally geek out and create a day-by-day chart to put on your bathroom mirror to track it.

- Are those goals realistic or do they need to be tweaked? Baby steps are better than no steps.

- How about the mental plan that you created? Did your ideas work in the heat of the spending moment or do those need to be reworked?

- Are there other situations you need to think through?

- What can you do better next week or next month?

- What is your reward if you meet your goals or hit a certain score for the month? Plan some kind of reward, keep it in front of you, and you will get there faster and have more fun along the way.

- Did you enlist your partner or friend to provide support?

The more time, effort, and focus you put into staying on top of this, the better your outcome. The speed at which you move in the direction of your ideal spending or your ideal balance sheet is up to you. You don't want to be miserable on the road to reaching your goals, so find a good balance, one that works for your life.

Repeat the whole process again: Evaluate, rate yourself, set new goals, tweak your strategies, execute on your plan, reward successes, and strategize over missteps. Do it over and over until you are a gazillionnaire!

Next up: Long-term goals are all about the fantasies, the deep desires, and the dreams you have for your life.

SECTION 2: Long-Term Goals

The Fun Stuff

If you are firmly in control of your cash flow and working toward your short-term balance sheet goals, then it's time to do some dreaming. This is the time to focus on the desires of your heart, not on reality.

Get out a piece of paper and fold it in half, length-wise. On the left side write, "things to own" and on the right side write, "things to experience" (or you can use the following list). Write down everything you can think of right now that you want to own or do. Go crazy; let your mind and your imagination go wild. Get it all down. Go!

Things to own	Things to experience

The Process of Getting What You Want

1. Identify what you want.

2. Determine when you want it.

3. Identify all of the things that have to happen for you to get it.

4. Determine when you will take each of the action steps listed in #3.

5. Identify what you need to learn or do as well as resources and information to help you along the way.

6. Work the list.

In the exercise above you identified a lot of potential medium-term and long-term desires/goals. Some of these will be a passing fancy, and you will never actually turn them into a goal that you purposely work to achieve, while others may stay on this list for many years. Regardless, most likely, every item on your list requires some amount of money. That's why this is all part of the financial planning process, which involves creating the plan for how you allocate your financial resources to get what you want while you take care of what you need.

Steps 1 and 2: Identify what you want and when you want it

Turn your brainstorming list from the first exercise into a goals list by evaluating how important each item is and when you want to achieve it. Write the goals in the chart below to determine how urgently you want to accomplish them and how realistic it might be to achieve them within that time frame.

One – Three Years	Three – Five Years	Five – 10 Years	> 10 Years

Look at the one to three years list. Read through the items on the list and rank them in order of importance; put 1, 2, 3 next to each one. Do the same for the remaining lists. Put some real thought into this. Sleep on it, discuss it with your spouse, and come up with what you feel in your gut is the number one priority for each of those time frames.

Steps 3 through 5: Determine what you need to make it happen

Start with the number one priority from the one to three years list, and write down all of the things that would have to happen for you to obtain or experience your item: what you might have to learn or research to complete that step, and who might be able to help. Then complete the rest of the columns similarly.

Example: Highest priority goal in the next one to three years is: Buying a house.

Most important because: I don't like living in an apartment and I want to build equity in an asset.

What do I have to do or achieve to make this a reality?	When do I need to complete this action step?	What do I need to know/learn/ do to complete this step?	How can I get information or help to complete this?
▪ Pay off all of my credit cards	▪ Prior to trying to qualify for the mortgage	▪ Create a strategic plan for paying down debt ▪ Create a budget ▪ Implement the plan, monitor progress regularly	▪ Complete the short-term goals section of this book and work through my spending plan to project how long it will take

What do I have to do or achieve to make this a reality?	When do I need to complete this action step?	What do I need to know/learn/ do to complete this step?	How can I get information or help to complete this?
• Pay off my student loans	• Prior to trying to qualify for the mortgage	• Create a strategic plan for paying down debt • Implement the plan, monitor progress regularly	• Complete the short-term goals section of this book and work through my spending plan to project how long it will take
• Save the down payment	• Prior to trying to qualify for the mortgage	• Create a strategic plan for saving money toward this goal	• Complete the short-term goals section of this book and work through my spending plan to project how long it will take
• Figure out how much house I can afford	• Anytime	• Read Chapter 9 and go through the calculations based on my projected income and debt	• Review Chapter 9 or online calculators
• Figure out what area of town I would like to live in that I can afford	• Anytime	• Drive around town, check online for housing prices in different areas	• Talk to people who live in different areas • Make a list of factors important to me

What do I have to do or achieve to make this a reality?	When do I need to complete this action step?	What do I need to know/learn/ do to complete this step?	How can I get information or help to complete this?
• Get my credit score above 700	• Prior to trying to qualify for the mortgage	• Find out what my credit score is currently • Correct any issues on my report • Research ways to increase my credit score • Develop a plan to do the recommended things	• Look at online resources
• Consider if I would have a roommate to reduce my costs	• Anytime	• Make a list of the pros and cons of having a roommate • Think about people I know and consider how I would feel about sharing my house with someone	• Talk to other people who are "landlords" and discuss pros and cons • Look online for comments from others in this situation
• Understand how to qualify for a mortgage loan	• Anytime	• Read Chapter 9 • Look at online resources	• Talk with a friend in that industry to get tips, as well as friends who have gone through the process

This is but one example of a common goal and how you might analyze it. Your list will probably be different, but hopefully you get the idea. This approach makes achieving the goal more concrete and gives you a checklist of actions that you can start working on today to move you toward that goal. It also keeps you focused when competing temptations arise. Now, go to the template and complete your own plan.

My highest priority goal in the next one to three years is:

_____

This is the most important thing to me because:

_____

What do I have to do or achieve to make this a reality?	When do I need to complete this action step?	What do I need to know/learn/ do to complete this step?	How can I get information or help to complete this?

Step 6: Work the list

Pick one of the items on your list and take one small step toward doing it. Set up a folder (paper or computer) to store relevant information, articles, your notes about the process, and actions you have taken.

Part of working the list is adding steps and revising the ones you already have. Information leads to more things you have to do that you didn't even know you had to do. That's just how it works. Sometimes information also leads to you realizing that this path isn't right for you. Perhaps you research house maintenance and think, "Yuck, I'd rather just call the apartment manager when things break." That's great; better to know that now than two months after buying the house.

A change in your circumstances could lead to a change of mind about your goals. Perhaps you take a job that involves moving to Europe for a couple of years. Time to bag the house goal and focus on some travel goals. What truly matters is the journey, not the destination, because the skills, confidence, and knowledge you gain in the process is where the value lies.

And on to the next goal . . .

You can create these kinds of planners for all of your goals, the top goal in each time frame, or just stay focused on one. This process is also effective for work goals, such as getting a promotion or completing a project. Even for a goal 10 years in the future, you have to take action today to get on the path toward that goal.

The next section covers protecting what you have. This is really quick and easy, so take a look to make sure you are "covered."

SECTION 3: Protecting Yourself and Your Family

You have done very well to get this far in the planning process. This is a quick but important section, so finish strong.

Risk management refers to the process of identifying risks that can hurt you, or in this case, hurt your financial plan, and making a plan to manage those risks. Risk management is an integral part of the financial planning process because some things could wipe you out financially if they were to occur. There are four courses of action to consider when examining risk: (1) assume the risk, (2) eliminate or avoid the risk, (3) mitigate (lessen) the risk, or (4) pass the risk of loss on to someone else (an insurance company). You will probably do a combination of these.

Consider the risk of your car being damaged in an accident.

- You could wing it and hope for the best (not legally an option in most states because your friends on the road need to be protected from you).

- You could keep your car in the garage and eliminate the risk of an accident (not practical, but effective).

- You could mitigate the risk of an accident by driving carefully, yielding to the crazy drivers, going the speed limit, eliminating distractions (cell phone), not eating while driving, driving sober, etc. (pretty effective, but not 100 percent).

- You could pass the risk on to an insurance company since these other options can't completely protect you from damage to your car, and losing your car to an accident would be financially disastrous for most (this is what most responsible people do).

Chapter 2 mentioned insurance with respect to your job, and in Chapter 7 you learned about the various types of insurance. Now, it's time to do an insurance review to be sure that you are covered for life's biggest risks.

Complete the following table of your insurance coverage.

Type of insurance	Deductible amount	Maximum benefit	Premium	Premium period
Health				
Dental				
Disability				
Auto				

Renter/ homeowner				
Life	NA			

You may not require life insurance if you are single and don't have children or other people who depend on your income to provide for their support. The other insurance types should definitely be on your radar if you don't have them. There are a few blank lines included in case you have more than one life policy (say, a group policy through work and an individual policy), or you may be required to have flood insurance or hurricane insurance if you live in high-risk areas.

As you look at your insurance, answer these questions:

- Are my coverages sufficient to cover potential losses?
- Do I have the savings to cover the deductible in the event of a loss?
- If I do have the deductible saved, could I increase the deductible even more to lower the premium?
- Is my auto coverage sufficient?
- Is my renters/homeowners insurance sufficient to replace all of my belongings if they were destroyed?
- Do I need life insurance?
- If I do, is the death benefit sufficient to provide for my dependents?

Keep in mind that you can discuss your coverages with your insurance agent at any time to be sure your coverage is adequate and to get details on how the premium would change if you made adjustments to the deductibles. You can also get quotes online to compare rates.

Insurance To-Dos

- If you are sufficiently covered, be sure you have all of your insurance contracts somewhere that you can easily get to them. Scan them so you also have the electronic copy. Be sure you back-up your hard drive frequently.

- Keep details about who to contact and what to do in the event you have a loss. What information would you need in order to report that loss?

- If you are married, be sure your spouse also has the details about who to contact.

- Set a calendar appointment with yourself to review your insurance annually to determine if you need to make changes.

- If you are not sufficiently covered, make a plan to get covered. Use the table below to itemize your tasks, set deadlines, and get it done.

If you have your own business, speak with an agent who specializes in small business insurance. You may need special coverages if you work out of your home, as your homeowner's insurance may not cover things like inventory and business equipment.

It isn't a financial plan without a plan of action. In the table below, indicate your action items:

Insurance type	Action needed	Date and time to complete it	Who to contact	Phone number or website

Estate Planning

With the estate tax exemption now at more than $5 million per person, most of us don't have to do much estate planning in the traditional sense (avoiding estate taxes), but everyone needs to plan for the worst, and needs to have the legal documents in place to handle such contingencies. These documents were mentioned in Chapter 11. Now is the time to review them and make a plan.

Health Care Directive

- Do you have one for the state you currently live in? If you have one for a previous state of residence, it may not be valid in your new state.

- Does it still reflect your wishes regarding your health care representative, your desires in the event of mental and physical incapacitation, and your desires in the event of terminal illness?

- Have you given a copy of it to your personal representative and other important family members?

Financial Power of Attorney

- Do you have one for the state you currently live in? If you have one for a previous state of residence, it may not be valid in your new state.

- Does it still reflect your wishes regarding who will act on your behalf (the person you granted power of attorney to)?

- Have you given a copy of it to your appointee?

Last Will and Testament

- If you don't have one, do you need a will? You do if you have children or other dependents who need a guardian appointed in the event of your death, if you have definite wishes regarding who will inherit your property (or who should not), or if you want to be sure that a particular person will handle your estate after your death (your executor).

- If you do have one, does it reference the state you currently live in? If you have one for a previous state of residence, it may not be valid (or portions may not) in your new state.

- If you do have one, does it still reflect your wishes regarding who will serve as your executor, who will be the beneficiaries, and when they will receive their inheritance?
- Have you given a copy to your executor (or at least provided details as to where the executor would get a copy in the event of your death)?
- Do you have an annual reminder to review your documents to be sure they are still valid?

Again, if there are holes in your estate plan, you need a plan to fill them. Fill in the details below:

Document type	Action needed	Date and time to complete it	Who to contact	Phone number or website

Remember, any time you have a life change, you need to consider whether your estate plan should be updated. Certainly, if you get married or divorced, you need to review all of your estate documents and your IRAs, 401(k)s, and life insurance to update beneficiaries. If you have a child, after you get the crib and the car seat, you need a guardian update to your will (and probably more life insurance).

One last thing, create an Estate Summary (see next page). Keep a copy for yourself in a safe place, and give another copy to your spouse, parents, or others who need to know in the event that something happens to you.

Now you have a financial plan. Go forth and implement it. You have all you need to make it happen. Be sure to revisit, review, and course correct as you go.

Estate Summary for

Name: _____

Date: _____

Health Care Directive dated _____

Health Care Representative _____

Alternate _____

Document can be found _____

Document prepared by (attorney's name or firm) _____

_____

Others who have a copy _____

_____

Durable Power of Attorney dated _____

Personal Representative _____

_____

Alternate _____

_____

Document can be found _____

Document prepared by (attorney's name or firm) _____

_____

Others who have a copy _____

_____

Last Will & Testament dated _____

Executor _____

Alternate Executor _____

Guardian _____

Alternate Guardian _____

Primary Beneficiary _____

Contingent Beneficiary _____

Document can be found _____

Document prepared by (attorney's name or firm) _____

Others who have a copy _____

Special terms _____

_____

_____

Life Insurance policy with _____

Primary Beneficiary: _____

Contingent Beneficiary: _____

Policy can be found _____

Death benefit amount _____

Group life policy through work: Yes/No, amount _____

Beneficiary _____

Retirement accounts:

401(k) through (employer name) _____

Custodian or plan administrator _____

Beneficiary _____

IRA account held by _____

Beneficiary _____

Roth IRA account held by _____

Beneficiary _____

Primary bank accounts (checking/savings) at _____

My passwords for online access can be found: _____

Other information that others should know: _____

_____

_____

_____

_____

Appendix:
A Bit About Financial Advisors

There are a lot of financial advisors in the marketplace today, and they range from insurance agents to accountants to investment brokers to attorneys. They all have their specialties and predispositions. If you go to an advisor based out of say, Northwestern Mutual Life, your recommendations will have a high bias toward insurance and annuity products. If you go to a Merrill Lynch-based advisor, you will get a high bias toward investment products. You should know the expertise or specialization of each advisor so that you understand where they may be biased.

Here are a few professional designations and what they mean:

CPA – Certified Public Accountant. These professionals know a lot about accounting, taxes, and financial statement preparation. They must pass a rigorous exam and have two years of experience working for a CPA to get certified. A CPA is a must-have for a small business owner unless you have a background in the accounting/tax arena. Note that someone can be a CPA and not know much about personal income tax if they specialize in audit, financial statement preparation, or corporate taxes, so you have to look at the person's specialty.

CFP® – CERTIFIED FINANCIAL PLANNER®. These folks have a well-rounded background in all personal financial areas: taxes, insurance, retirement planning, college planning, estate planning, and investment management. They must pass a rigorous exam covering all of these areas, as well as general economics, and must have three years of experience in financial planning to become certified. Find a CFP® to help you with any type of comprehensive financial plan. Everything interconnects and impacts taxes, so you want the big picture view. A CFP® should take a holistic view of your financial life and can probably refer you to other professionals who may be needed, such as attorneys or tax preparers. Be aware, though, even CFPs® have their specialties, so be sure to ask.

CFA – Chartered Financial Analyst. These experts must pass an exam and have relevant educational and work experience to become certified. CFAs have extensive knowledge of investments and other financial analysis, so they may be totally focused on the investment aspect of your financial life.

CAS® – Certified Annuity Specialist®. Guess what these people specialize in? Right, annuities. Annuities are insurance contracts that provide a cash flow stream based on the criteria identified. If you know you need an annuity, this would be a great person to contact, but annuities are a very specialized product, so they are definitely not for everybody.

CLU - Certified Life Underwriter. These folks are specialists in life insurance. If you go to a professional with CLU behind his or her name, you will get a bias toward insurance products and possibly annuities.

There are dozens more financial and insurance designations. If you see letters behind someone's name on their business card, and you don't recognize the designation, ask what it means. You should understand what their specialty is, as not all financial advisors have the same educational training and professional experience.

The important thing is to identify what you need and make sure that the financial advisor you choose can meet those needs.

Fee-Only Versus Commission-Based Advisors

Fee-only means that the person gets paid only based on the fee that he or she charges you for either financial planning (usually a flat fee), financial consulting (hourly or flat fee), or asset management (a percentage based on the assets managed for you).

The contrast is a professional who gets paid on commission. The stock brokers of old are a good example of a commission-based advisor.

They don't get paid unless you buy a product that they recommend. They may say that you don't pay a fee, but make no mistake, you are paying; you just pay on the buy or sell of a security or other financial products.

There are many good, upstanding professionals who operate under this model (and in insurance, this is the only model); however, one problem that arises is the conflict of interest between what is good for you and how much commission the advisor will make. It's easy for advisors to convince themselves that product A is fantastic when, in fact, they make twice as much commission on it as they make on product B. That's just human nature.

Everyone needs to get paid for their work and for their expertise, and the model that keeps the financial planner's interest aligned with the client's interest is the fee-only planner. You can find out more about fee-only planners on the National Association of Personal Financial Advisors website, www.napfa.org. You can search for fee-only advisors in your area, as well as get more information about services. The CFP Board® website has an advisor lookup feature. They have a national campaign to help the general public find CFP planners and launched www.letsmakeaplan.org to help people connect with qualified planners.

If you plan to interview a financial advisor, you should interview at least two or three advisors to get a feel for:

- what they do;
- what their specialty is;
- whether you are a good fit for their firm (do their other clients have the same type of profile as you do?); and
- what biases they may have (i.e., toward insurance versus investment products versus creating a financial plan).

You should also

- Ask for references, and then call or email them to ask about their experience.
- Review the advisor's website.

- Understand who regulates financial advisors (an insurance commissioner, the SEC, FINRA, etc.) and understand what standards they are bound by.

- Trust your gut and make sure you feel comfortable talking with the advisor.

- Understand exactly how much you are paying in fees and what you are getting for that fee.

- Know if the advisor is a fiduciary or not. A fee-only advisor is a fiduciary but brokers and insurance agents are not.

- Know if your financial manager has your money or if it is held by a third-party custodian. Bernie Madoff had his clients' money (and he took it). A custodian is much more secure; the advisor has the authority to place investment trades but not withdraw the money.

- Ask about the risk involved in the investment portfolio (historic volatility) and the liquidity of the investments. Investing in illiquid securities carries more risk and makes it harder to get your money out if you need it.

- Read the contract and ask questions if you don't understand what something means.

- Communicate, communicate, communicate with the advisor. An advisor can't meet your needs if he or she doesn't know what they are. If you aren't getting what you need, say so. You can be tactful, but make your priorities, concerns, or issues clear.

Appendix: I-9 Employment Eligibility Verification

Employment Eligibility Verification

Department of Homeland Security
U.S. Citizenship and Immigration Services

**USCIS
Form I-9**
OMB No. 1615-0047
Expires 03/31/2016

▶START HERE. Read instructions carefully before completing this form. The instructions must be available during completion of this form.
ANTI-DISCRIMINATION NOTICE: It is illegal to discriminate against work-authorized individuals. Employers **CANNOT** specify which document(s) they will accept from an employee. The refusal to hire an individual because the documentation presented has a future expiration date may also constitute illegal discrimination.

Section 1. Employee Information and Attestation *(Employees must complete and sign Section 1 of Form I-9 no later than the* **first day of employment***, but not before accepting a job offer.)*

Last Name *(Family Name)*	First Name *(Given Name)*	Middle Initial	Other Names Used *(if any)*

Address *(Street Number and Name)*	Apt. Number	City or Town	State	Zip Code

Date of Birth *(mm/dd/yyyy)*	U.S. Social Security Number	E-mail Address	Telephone Number

I am aware that federal law provides for imprisonment and/or fines for false statements or use of false documents in connection with the completion of this form.

I attest, under penalty of perjury, that I am (check one of the following):

☐ A citizen of the United States

☐ A noncitizen national of the United States *(See instructions)*

☐ A lawful permanent resident (Alien Registration Number/USCIS Number): _____

☐ An alien authorized to work until (expiration date, if applicable, mm/dd/yyyy) _____ Some aliens may write "N/A" in this field.
(See instructions)

For aliens authorized to work, provide your Alien Registration Number/USCIS Number **OR** *Form I-94 Admission Number:*

1. Alien Registration Number/USCIS Number: _____

OR

2. Form I-94 Admission Number: _____

   If you obtained your admission number from CBP in connection with your arrival in the United States, include the following:

   Foreign Passport Number: _____

   Country of Issuance: _____

   Some aliens may write "N/A" on the Foreign Passport Number and Country of Issuance fields. *(See instructions)*

3-D Barcode
Do Not Write in This Space

Signature of Employee:	Date *(mm/dd/yyyy)*:

Preparer and/or Translator Certification *(To be completed and signed if Section 1 is prepared by a person other than the employee.)*

I attest, under penalty of perjury, that I have assisted in the completion of this form and that to the best of my knowledge the information is true and correct.

Signature of Preparer or Translator:	Date *(mm/dd/yyyy)*:

Last Name *(Family Name)*	First Name *(Given Name)*

Address *(Street Number and Name)*	City or Town	State	Zip Code

🛑 *Employer Completes Next Page* 🛑

Section 2. Employer or Authorized Representative Review and Verification

(Employers or their authorized representative must complete and sign Section 2 within 3 business days of the employee's first day of employment. You must physically examine one document from List A OR examine a combination of one document from List B and one document from List C as listed on the "Lists of Acceptable Documents" on the next page of this form. For each document you review, record the following information: document title, issuing authority, document number, and expiration date, if any.)

Employee Last Name, First Name and Middle Initial from Section 1:

List A	OR	List B	AND	List C
Identity and Employment Authorization		Identity		Employment Authorization

List A	List B	List C
Document Title:	Document Title:	Document Title:
Issuing Authority:	Issuing Authority:	Issuing Authority:
Document Number:	Document Number:	Document Number:
Expiration Date *(if any)(mm/dd/yyyy)*:	Expiration Date *(if any)(mm/dd/yyyy)*:	Expiration Date *(if any)(mm/dd/yyyy)*:
Document Title:		
Issuing Authority:		
Document Number:		
Expiration Date *(if any)(mm/dd/yyyy)*:		
Document Title:		3-D Barcode
Issuing Authority:		Do Not Write in This Space
Document Number:		
Expiration Date *(if any)(mm/dd/yyyy)*:		

Certification

I attest, under penalty of perjury, that (1) I have examined the document(s) presented by the above-named employee, (2) the above-listed document(s) appear to be genuine and to relate to the employee named, and (3) to the best of my knowledge the employee is authorized to work in the United States.

The employee's first day of employment *(mm/dd/yyyy)* _____ *(See instructions for exemptions.)*

Signature of Employer or Authorized Representative	Date *(mm/dd/yyyy)*	Title of Employer or Authorized Representative
Last Name *(Family Name)*	First Name *(Given Name)*	Employer's Business or Organization Name
Employer's Business or Organization Address *(Street Number and Name)*	City or Town	State	Zip Code

Section 3. Reverification and Rehires *(To be completed and signed by employer or authorized representative.)*

A. New Name *(if applicable)* Last Name *(Family Name)* First Name *(Given Name)*	Middle Initial	B. Date of Rehire *(if applicable) (mm/dd/yyyy)*

C. If employee's previous grant of employment authorization has expired, provide the information for the document from List A or List C the employee presented that establishes current employment authorization in the space provided below.

Document Title:	Document Number:	Expiration Date *(if any)(mm/dd/yyyy)*:

I attest, under penalty of perjury, that to the best of my knowledge, this employee is authorized to work in the United States, and if the employee presented document(s), the document(s) I have examined appear to be genuine and to relate to the individual.

Signature of Employer or Authorized Representative:	Date *(mm/dd/yyyy)*:	Print Name of Employer or Authorized Representative:

Appendix: Form W-4 Employee's Withholding Allowance Certificate

Form W-4 (2014)

Purpose. Complete Form W-4 so that your employer can withhold the correct federal income tax from your pay. Consider completing a new Form W-4 each year and when your personal or financial situation changes.

Exemption from withholding. If you are exempt, complete only lines 1, 2, 3, 4, and 7 and sign the form to validate it. Your exemption for 2014 expires February 17, 2015. See Pub. 505, Tax Withholding and Estimated Tax.

Note. If another person can claim you as a dependent on his or her tax return, you cannot claim exemption if your income exceeds $1,000 and includes more than $350 of unearned income (for example, interest and dividends).

Exceptions An employee may be able to claim exemption from withholding even if the employee is a dependent, if the employee:
• Is age 65 or older,
• Is blind, or
• Will claim adjustments to income; tax credits; or itemized deductions, on his or her tax return.

The exceptions do not apply to supplemental wages greater than $1,000,000.

Basic instructions. If you are not exempt, complete the Personal Allowances Worksheet below. The worksheets on page 2 further adjust your withholding allowances based on itemized deductions, certain credits, adjustments to income, or two-earners/multiple jobs situations.

Complete all worksheets that apply. However, you may claim fewer (or zero) allowances. For regular wages, withholding must be based on allowances you claimed and may not be a flat amount or percentage of wages.

Head of household. Generally, you can claim head of household filing status on your tax return only if you are unmarried and pay more than 50% of the costs of keeping up a home for yourself and your dependent(s) or other qualifying individuals. See Pub. 501, Exemptions, Standard Deduction, and Filing Information, for information.

Tax credits. You can take projected tax credits into account in figuring your allowable number of withholding allowances. Credits for child or dependent care expenses and the child tax credit may be claimed using the Personal Allowances Worksheet below. See Pub. 505 for information on converting your other credits into withholding allowances.

Nonwage income. If you have a large amount of nonwage income, such as interest or dividends, consider making estimated tax payments using Form 1040-ES, Estimated Tax for Individuals. Otherwise, you may owe additional tax. If you have pension or annuity income, see Pub. 505 to find out if you should adjust your withholding on Form W-4 or W-4P.

Two earners or multiple jobs. If you have a working spouse or more than one job, figure the total number of allowances you are entitled to claim on all jobs using worksheets from only one Form W-4. Your withholding usually will be most accurate when all allowances are claimed on the Form W-4 for the highest paying job and zero allowances are claimed on the others. See Pub. 505 for details.

Nonresident alien. If you are a nonresident alien, see Notice 1392, Supplemental Form W-4 Instructions for Nonresident Aliens, before completing this form.

Check your withholding. After your Form W-4 takes effect, use Pub. 505 to see how the amount you are having withheld compares to your projected total tax for 2014. See Pub. 505, especially if your earnings exceed $130,000 (Single) or $180,000 (Married).

Future developments. Information about any future developments affecting Form W-4 (such as legislation enacted after we release it) will be posted at www.irs.gov/w4.

Personal Allowances Worksheet (Keep for your records.)

A   Enter "1" for **yourself** if no one else can claim you as a dependent . . . . A _____

B   Enter "1" if: { • You are single and have only one job; or
  • You are married, have only one job, and your spouse does not work; or   } . . . . B _____
  • Your wages from a second job or your spouse's wages (or the total of both) are $1,500 or less.

C   Enter "1" for your **spouse**. But, you may choose to enter "-0-" if you are married and have either a working spouse or more than one job. (Entering "-0-" may help you avoid having too little tax withheld.) . . . . C _____

D   Enter number of **dependents** (other than your spouse or yourself) you will claim on your tax return . . . . D _____

E   Enter "1" if you will file as **head of household** on your tax return (see conditions under **Head of household** above) . . E _____

F   Enter "1" if you have at least $2,000 of **child or dependent care expenses** for which you plan to claim a credit . . F _____
  (**Note.** Do **not** include child support payments. See Pub. 503, Child and Dependent Care Expenses, for details.)

G   **Child Tax Credit** (including additional child tax credit). See Pub. 972, Child Tax Credit, for more information.
  • If your total income will be less than $65,000 ($95,000 if married), enter "2" for each eligible child; then **less** "1" if you
  have three to six eligible children or **less** "2" if you have seven or more eligible children.
  • If your total income will be between $65,000 and $84,000 ($95,000 and $119,000 if married), enter "1" for each eligible child . . . G _____

H   Add lines A through G and enter total here. (**Note.** This may be different from the number of exemptions you claim on your tax return.) ► H _____

For accuracy, complete all worksheets that apply.
• If you plan to **itemize** or **claim adjustments to income** and want to reduce your withholding, see the **Deductions and Adjustments Worksheet** on page 2.
• If you are **single** and have more than **one job** or are **married** and you and your spouse both work and the combined earnings from all jobs exceed $50,000 ($20,000 if married), see the **Two-Earners/Multiple Jobs Worksheet** on page 2 to avoid having too little tax withheld.
• If **neither** of the above situations applies, **stop here** and enter the number from line H on line 5 of Form W-4 below.

-------- Separate here and give Form W-4 to your employer. Keep the top part for your records. --------

---

Form W-4
Department of the Treasury
Internal Revenue Service

Employee's Withholding Allowance Certificate

► Whether you are entitled to claim a certain number of allowances or exemption from withholding is subject to review by the IRS. Your employer may be required to send a copy of this form to the IRS.

OMB No. 1545-0074

2014

1 Your first name and middle initial Last name	2 Your social security number

Home address (number and street or rural route)

City or town, state, and ZIP code

3 ☐ Single   ☐ Married   ☐ Married, but withhold at higher Single rate.
Note. If married, but legally separated, or spouse is a nonresident alien, check the "Single" box.

4   If your last name differs from that shown on your social security card,
check here. You must call 1-800-772-1213 for a replacement card. ► ☐

5   Total number of allowances you are claiming (from line H above **or** from the applicable worksheet on page 2)   **5** _____

6   Additional amount, if any, you want withheld from each paycheck . . . . **6** $ _____

7   I claim exemption from withholding for 2014, and I certify that I meet **both** of the following conditions for exemption.
  • Last year I had a right to a refund of **all** federal income tax withheld because I had **no** tax liability, **and**
  • This year I expect a refund of **all** federal income tax withheld because I expect to have **no** tax liability.
  If you meet both conditions, write "Exempt" here . . . . ► **7** _____

Under penalties of perjury, I declare that I have examined this certificate and, to the best of my knowledge and belief, it is true, correct, and complete.

Employee's signature
(This form is not valid unless you sign it.) ►   Date ►

8 Employer's name and address (Employer: Complete lines 8 and 10 only if sending to the IRS.)	9 Office code (optional)	10 Employer identification number (EIN)

For Privacy Act and Paperwork Reduction Act Notice, see page 2.   Cat. No. 10220Q   Form **W-4** (2014)

Form W-4 (2014)

Page **2**

Deductions and Adjustments Worksheet

Note. Use this worksheet *only* if you plan to itemize deductions or claim certain credits or adjustments to income.

1	Enter an estimate of your 2014 itemized deductions. These include qualifying home mortgage interest, charitable contributions, state and local taxes, medical expenses in excess of 10% (7.5% if either you or your spouse was born before January 2, 1950) of your income, and miscellaneous deductions. For 2014, you may have to reduce your itemized deductions if your income is over $305,050 and you are married filing jointly or are a qualifying widow(er); $279,650 if you are head of household; $254,200 if you are single and not head of household or a qualifying widow(er); or $152,525 if you are married filing separately. See Pub. 505 for details	1	$
2	Enter: { $12,400 if married filing jointly or qualifying widow(er) / $9,100 if head of household / $6,200 if single or married filing separately }	2	$
3	**Subtract** line 2 from line 1. If zero or less, enter "-0-"	3	$
4	Enter an estimate of your 2014 adjustments to income and any additional standard deduction (see Pub. 505)	4	$
5	**Add** lines 3 and 4 and enter the total. (Include any amount for credits from the *Converting Credits to Withholding Allowances for 2014 Form W-4* worksheet in Pub. 505.)	5	$
6	Enter an estimate of your 2014 nonwage income (such as dividends or interest)	6	$
7	**Subtract** line 6 from line 5. If zero or less, enter "-0-"	7	$
8	**Divide** the amount on line 7 by $3,950 and enter the result here. Drop any fraction	8	
9	Enter the number from the **Personal Allowances Worksheet**, line H, page 1	9	
10	**Add** lines 8 and 9 and enter the total here. If you plan to use the **Two-Earners/Multiple Jobs Worksheet**, also enter this total on line 1 below. Otherwise, **stop here** and enter this total on Form W-4, line 5, page 1	10	

Two-Earners/Multiple Jobs Worksheet (See *Two earners or multiple jobs* on page 1.)

Note. Use this worksheet *only* if the instructions under line H on page 1 direct you here.

1	Enter the number from line H, page 1 (or from line 10 above if you used the **Deductions and Adjustments Worksheet**)	1	
2	Find the number in **Table 1** below that applies to the **LOWEST** paying job and enter it here. **However**, if you are married filing jointly and wages from the highest paying job are $65,000 or less, do not enter more than "3"	2	
3	If line 1 is **more than or equal to** line 2, subtract line 2 from line 1. Enter the result here (if zero, enter "-0-") and on Form W-4, line 5, page 1. **Do not** use the rest of this worksheet	3	

Note. If line 1 is **less than** line 2, enter "-0-" on Form W-4, line 5, page 1. Complete lines 4 through 9 below to figure the additional withholding amount necessary to avoid a year-end tax bill.

4	Enter the number from line 2 of this worksheet	4	
5	Enter the number from line 1 of this worksheet	5	
6	**Subtract** line 5 from line 4	6	
7	Find the amount in **Table 2** below that applies to the **HIGHEST** paying job and enter it here	7	$
8	**Multiply** line 7 by line 6 and enter the result here. This is the additional annual withholding needed	8	$
9	Divide line 8 by the number of pay periods remaining in 2014. For example, divide by 25 if you are paid every two weeks and you complete this form on a date in January when there are 25 pay periods remaining in 2014. Enter the result here and on Form W-4, line 6, page 1. This is the additional amount to be withheld from each paycheck	9	$

Table 1

Married Filing Jointly		All Others	
If wages from **LOWEST** paying job are—	Enter on line 2 above	If wages from **LOWEST** paying job are—	Enter on line 2 above
$0 - $6,000	0	$0 - $6,000	0
6,001 - 13,000	1	6,001 - 16,000	1
13,001 - 24,000	2	16,001 - 25,000	2
24,001 - 26,000	3	25,001 - 34,000	3
26,001 - 33,000	4	34,001 - 43,000	4
33,001 - 43,000	5	43,001 - 70,000	5
43,001 - 49,000	6	70,001 - 85,000	6
49,001 - 60,000	7	85,001 - 110,000	7
60,001 - 75,000	8	110,001 - 125,000	8
75,001 - 80,000	9	125,001 - 140,000	9
80,001 - 100,000	10	140,001 and over	10
100,001 - 115,000	11		
115,001 - 130,000	12		
130,001 - 140,000	13		
140,001 - 150,000	14		
150,001 and over	15		

Table 2

Married Filing Jointly		All Others	
If wages from **HIGHEST** paying job are—	Enter on line 7 above	If wages from **HIGHEST** paying job are—	Enter on line 7 above
$0 - $74,000	$590	$0 - $37,000	$590
74,001 - 130,000	990	37,001 - 80,000	990
130,001 - 200,000	1,110	80,001 - 175,000	1,110
200,001 - 355,000	1,300	175,001 - 385,000	1,300
355,001 - 400,000	1,380	385,001 and over	1,560
400,001 and over	1,560		

Appendix: Health Insurance Comparison Worksheet

Health Insurance Comparison Summary

Plan option	Annual premium	Annual deductible	Co-Insurance percentage	Co-Insurance limit	Maximum out-of-pocket cost	Is what I need covered?	Exclusions that will impact me?	H.S.A. qualified?	Cost under "best case" scenario	Cost under "worst case" scenario

Appendix: Resources

If you need to change your beliefs, there are lots of books on this concept. *As A Man Thinketh* was one of the first to talk about how your thoughts control your actions. It is a short book, written a long time ago, so the language (as in "thinketh") is a little old-fashioned, but the concept is timeless. For an ultra-new spin on how thoughts impact your actions, check out Mike Dooley's *Notes From the Universe* books or Google TUT's Adventure Club and sign up for his daily "TUT ...Thoughts From the Universe" email for some inspiration. His tagline, "Thoughts become things . . . choose the good ones" says it all.

Debbie Ford's *The Dark Side of the Light Chasers* is another great book that deals with self-esteem beliefs such as "I don't deserve success or wealth" and how similar subconscious beliefs (the dark side) cause you to sabotage yourself.

Hyrum Smith, co-founder of the Franklin Planner, has done a lot of work in the area of changing beliefs. He uses the concept of the "belief window" to think about the impact that beliefs have on actions. Find him on YouTube, or at his website www.hyrumwsmith.com, or take a look at his book, *The Power of Perception*.

If habits are your issue, read *The Power of Habit* by Charles Duhigg. This is a super interesting book about habits, how we get them, change them, and effectively use them. His website, www.charlesduhigg.com has loads of resources.

If you need to work on giving up on the blame game, try resources by these giants in the personal empowerment arena:

- Anthony Robbins
- Brian Tracy
- Dr. Wayne Dyer
- Zig Ziglar (sales, especially)
- Og Mandino (also big for folks in sales – which is everyone)
- Denis Waitley

You don't have to spend a dime on many of these resources. Most of these gurus have websites with free information. Of course, the library is packed with their books and audiobooks. You should definitely invest in your own personal development, but always try to get it free first!

And of course, check out www.graduatesguidetomoney.com for links, resources, and downloadable worksheets to get your beliefs in order.